Hands On Algebra

Table of Contents

Numbers

Equations

Coordinate Systems/Shapes

Games

TI-81 Graphing Calculator

Numbers

Basic Numbers...Just for Fun!

Name _____

OBJECTIVE: To review basic arithmetic in a fun manner

Fill in the crossnumber puzzle by solving the problems below.

Across

1.   347 + 962 + 384
4.   14 tens + 2
6.   11,538 – 3,472
7.   23 + 126 + 84 + 94
9.   4,256 – 3,257
12.   89 + 230 + 36 + 47
13.   632 – 582
14. $(2 \times 10^3) + (2 \times 10) + 5$
16.   1,057 – 73
17.   1,006 – 916
18.   one thousand eight hundred five
21.   3,000 – 2,973
22.   606 hundreds

Down

1.   6,766 – 4,927
2.   16 + 26 + 37 + 19
3.   3 hundreds
4.   163 x 100
5.   2 hundreds + 8 tens + 7
8.   10,214 – 7,985
10.   122 + 836
11. $(9 \times 10^3) + 40 + 1$
12.   32,000 + 10,000
15.   50 hundreds
16.   94 tens + 2
19.   13 + 9 + 14 + 26 + 24
20.   34,562 – 34,506

Measuring Problems

Name _____

OBJECTIVE: To use problem-solving skills to answer the questions below

Answer the questions below.

1. How can you cook an egg for exactly 15 minutes if all you have is a 7-minute hourglass and an 11-minute hourglass?

2. How can a 24-gallon can of water be divided evenly among three men using unmarked cans whose capacities are 5, 11 and 13 gallons?

3. Nine coins are in a bag. They all look alike but one is counterfeit. It weighs less than the others. Use a balance scale to find the fake coin in exactly two weighings.

4. Twelve coins are in a bag. They all look alike but one is counterfeit. It weighs less than the others. Use a balance scale to find the fake coin in exactly three weighings.

5. In each of the pictures below, the scales balance. How many boxes of popcorn does one can of soda weigh? You will need all of the pictures to answer the question.

3

You Write the Rules (Addition)

Name _____

OBJECTIVE: To develop rules for adding positive and negative numbers by grouping examples into patterns and analyzing those patterns

---

I. Add the following problems using the number line below and counting (tracing) with your finger.

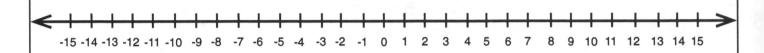

-15 -14 -13 -12 -11 -10 -9 -8 -7 -6 -5 -4 -3 -2 -1 0 1 2 3 4 5 6 7 8 9 10 11 12 13 14 15

Example:

-2 + 5 = __?__ .

 = 3

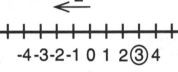

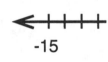

-15   -4 -3 -2 -1 0 1 2 ③ 4   15

↑
begin

So -2 + 5 = __3__ .

I'M POSITIVE THESE NEGATIVES WILL BE A POSITIVE EXPERIENCE!

1. -3 ___

2. 5 + 3 = _____

3. -2 + 7 = _____

4. 3 + -8 = _____

5. 15 + -15 = _____

6. -1 + 16 = _____

7. 13 + -11 = _____

8. 5 + -17 = _____

9. 3 + 6 = _____

10. -11 + -8 = _____

11. 1 + 11 = _____

12. -2 + -2 = _____

13. 10 + -8 = _____

14. -4 + -6 = _____

15. -8 + 2 = _____

Numbers

You Write the Rules
(Addition) continued

Name _____

OBJECTIVE: To develop rules for adding positive and negative numbers by grouping examples into patterns and analyzing those patterns

II. Group the problems from page 4 into "same signs" and "different signs."

	SAME	**DIFFERENT**
example	-3 + -4 = __-7__ .	-2 + 7 = __5__ .

III. Answer the following questions and analyze your responses to help you write a rule for each pattern.

1. In the "same" column,

a) how was the numerical part of the answer found (i.e. addition, subtraction, multiplication, division)? _____

_____

b) how was the sign determined? _____

_____

2. In the "different" column,

a) how was the numerical part of the answer found (i.e. addition, subtraction, multiplication, division)? _____

_____

b) how was the sign determined? _____

_____

3. Write a rule for each pattern describing how both the numerical part and the sign part of the answer were determined.

a) "When adding two numbers with the same sign _____

_____ ."

b) "When adding two numbers with different signs _____

_____ ."

You Write the Rules (Addition)

Name _____

OBJECTIVE: To use the rules developed for adding positive and negative numbers

A Solve each problem.

1. -8 + 2 = D
2. -3 + -4 = E
3. 10 + -32 = I
4. -27 + 86 = N
5. 7 + -20 = A
6. 8 + 9 = K
7. 5 + -5 = O
8. -1 + 4 = T
9. -9 + -14 = A
10. -3 + 5 = J

11. 113 + -105 = S
12. -16 + -77 = M
13. 20 + -30 = B
14. -285 + 198 = G
15. -165 + -92 = Q
16. -29 + 11 = R
17. -37 + -41 = V
18. 48 + -85 = F
19. 15 + -8 = C
20. 10 + -25 = R

21. -12 + -8 = W
22. -12 + 30 = S
23. -10 + 20 = P
24. -40 + -40 = X
25. 5 + -1 = H
26. -76 + -150 = L
27. 56 + 98 = Y
28. -12 + 61 = U
29. 4 + -7 = Z
30. -5 + 19 = H

B Finish the rules below. Put the letter from above next to the corresponding number below in order to read the complete rules.

1. When adding two numbers with the same sign...

| -13 | -6 | -6 | | -13 | 59 | -6 | | 17 | -7 | -7 | 10 |

| 3 | 4 | -7 | | 8 | -22 | -87 | 59 | • |

2. When adding two numbers with different signs...

| 8 | 49 | -10 | 3 | -15 | -13 | 7 | 3 | | -13 | 59 | -6 | | 3 | -13 | 17 | -7 |

| 3 | 4 | -7 | | 8 | -22 | -87 | 59 | | 0 | -37 | | 3 | 4 | -7 |

| -226 | -13 | -15 | -87 | -7 | -15 | | 59 | 49 | -18 | -10 | -7 | -15 | • |

You Write the Rules (Multiplication)

Numbers

Name _____

OBJECTIVE: To develop rules for multiplying positive and negative numbers

I. Given:

1. $3 \cdot 2 = 6$	6. $-3 \cdot -4 = 12$	11. $8 \cdot -8 = -64$
2. $-3 \cdot 2 = -6$	7. $-4 \cdot 3 = -12$	12. $7 \cdot -1 = -7$
3. $-5 \cdot -4 = 20$	8. $3 \cdot -4 = -12$	13. $5 \cdot 10 = 50$
4. $1 \cdot -7 = -7$	9. $-5 \cdot 4 = -20$	14. $2 \cdot 8 = 16$
5. $-3 \cdot 7 = -21$	10. $-7 \cdot 3 = -21$	15. $-2 \cdot -8 = 16$

Group the problems into "same signs" and "different signs."

	SAME	DIFFERENT
example	$3 \cdot 2 = 6$	$-3 \cdot 2 = -6$

II. Answer the following questions and analyze your responses to help you write a rule for each pattern.

1. In the "same" column,

   a) what is the sign of the answer in every example? _____

   b) does it matter which number is larger? _____

   c) does it matter which number is written first? _____

2. In the "different" column,

   a) what Is the sign of the answer in every example? _____

   b) does it matter which number is larger? _____

   c) does it matter which number is written first? _____

3. Write a rule for each pattern.

   a) When multiplying two numbers with the same sign, the answer will be _____ .

   b) When multiplying two numbers with different signs, the answer will be _____ .

7

You Write the Rules
(Division)

Name _____

OBJECTIVE: To use the rules developed for multiplying signed numbers and to extend these to discuss division of signed numbers

I. Recall that $\frac{6}{3} = 2$ or $\frac{6}{2} = 3$ because $2 \cdot 3 = 6$ and therefore $\frac{-6}{-3} = 2$ or $\frac{-6}{2} = -3$

for the same reason. Using this logic, go through the 15 examples on page 7 and rewrite each as a division sentence. Then, group your problems into "same" and "different" categories as before.

1. _____	6. _____	11. _____
2. _____	7. _____	12. _____
3. _____	8. _____	13. _____
4. _____	9. _____	14. _____
5. _____	10. _____	15. _____

	SAME	**DIFFERENT**
example	$\frac{6}{3} = 2$	$\frac{-6}{2} = -3$

II. Repeat the questions asked for multiplication. Write a rule for each pattern.

1. When dividing two numbers with the same sign, the answer will be _____ .

2. When dividing two numbers with different signs, the answer will be _____ .

You Write the Rules
(Multiplication and Division)

Name _____

OBJECTIVE: To use the rules developed for multiplying and dividing positive and negative numbers

A. The Multiplication Table

The multiplication table below has eight mistakes. Find each one and circle it. Write the corrected problems and answers going from top to bottom, left to right, in the spaces provided below.

x	3	-4	7	1	-8	-6	10	-1	2	5
-2	-6	8	14	-2	-16	12	-20	2	-4	-10
3	6	-12	21	3	-24	-18	-30	-3	5	15
-5	-15	20	-35	-5	40	-30	-50	5	-10	-25
-11	33	44	-77	-11	88	66	-110	11	-22	55

1. ____ x ____ = H   3. ____ x ____ = I   5. ____ x ____ = A   7. ____ x ____ = R

2. ____ x ____ = M   4. ____ x ____ = T   6. ____ x ____ = A   8. ____ x ____ = E

B. Division Practice

Solve the following problems.

1. $60 \div -15 =$ ____ S

2. $3 \div -3 =$ ____ F

3. $-48 \div 3 =$ ____ N

4. $300 \div 2 =$ ____ U

5. $-39 \div -3 =$ ____ D

6. $80 \div -40 =$ ____ K

7. $96 \div 12 =$ ____ Y

8. $56 \div -8 =$ ____ ,

9. $-63 \div -3 =$ ____ ?

10. $-38 \div -19 =$ ____ L

11. $-45 \div 3 =$ ____ O

12. $-91 \div -91 =$ ____ V

13. $\frac{-430}{-2} =$ ____ !

14. $\frac{-130}{-10} =$ ____ D

15. $\frac{-42}{3} =$ ____ I

16. $\frac{77}{77} =$ ____ V

17. $\frac{-49}{7} =$ ____ ,

18. $\frac{330}{-10} =$ ____ M

C. Put the letter corresponding to each answer above in the spaces below.

___ ___ ___ ___ ___   ___ ___ ___ ___   ___ ___   ___ ___ ___
-14 9 -55 30 6   -33 30 16 9   -14 -4   -1 150 -16

___ ___ ___   ___ ___ ___ ___ ___   ___ ___   ___ ___ ___
30 -16 13   -55 30 -4 8 -7   13 -15   8 -15 150

___ ___ ___ ___ ___   ___ ___ ___   ___   ___ ___ ___ ___   ___ ___ ___ ___ ___
16 9 -14 -16 -2   -4 -15 21   -14   2 -15 1 -55   -33 30 16 9 215

Other Rules for Addition/Subtraction/ Multiplication/Division

Numbers

Name _____

OBJECTIVE: To learn and use various rules for the basic operations of numbers

Name	Rule	What it all means!
Additive Identity	$a + 0 = a$	Adding zero to a number does not change its identity.
Multiplicative Identity	$a \cdot 1 = a$	Multiplying a number by one does not change its identity.
Additive Inverse	$a + (-a) = 0$	Numbers whose sum is zero (opposites)
Subtraction	$a - b = a + -b$	To subtract, add the opposite.
Zero Multiplication	$a \cdot 0 = 0$	Multiplying a number by zero gives a product of zero.
Multiplicative Inverse	$a \cdot \frac{1}{a} = 1$	Two numbers that when multiplied give a product of one (reciprocals)

1. Recall:

   a) When adding two numbers with the same sign, _____ _____ .

   b) When adding two numbers with different signs, _____ _____ .

2. Recall:

   a) When multiplying/dividing two numbers with the same sign, _____ _____ .

   b) When multiplying/dividing two numbers with different signs, _____ _____ .

3. Fill in the answer and the name of the identity for the following. Then, write your own example for each.

   a) $3 + 0 =$ _____, _____, _____ + _____ = _____

   b) $-5 \cdot \frac{-1}{5} =$ _____, _____, _____ + _____ = _____

   c) $-6 + 6 =$ _____, _____, _____ + _____ = _____

   d) $1 \cdot -17 =$ _____, _____, _____ + _____ = _____

   e) $5 - 3 = 5 + -3 =$ _____, _____, _____ + _____ = _____

   f) $71 \cdot 0 =$ _____, _____, _____ + _____ = _____

4. Recall order of operations:

   a) _____

   b) _____

   c) _____

10

Number Practice

Name _____

OBJECTIVE: To combine and use all rules for operations with numbers

Simplify.

1. $-76 + -150$ = _____

2. $-9 + 87$ = _____

3. $-3 + 5$ = _____

4. $-25 + 25$ = _____

5. $-16 + -77$ = _____

6. $54 + -73$ = _____

7. $7 - -4$ = _____

8. $700 - -77$ = _____

9. $-4 + -25$ = _____

10. $57 \bullet -9$ = _____

11. $-7 + 0$ = _____

12. $(25)(-25)$ = _____

13. $-48 \div 3$ = _____

14. $^{100}/_{20}$ = _____

15. $45 \div -9$ = _____

16. $(-5)(24)$ = _____

17. $-10 \bullet -30$ = _____

18. $36 \div -2$ = _____

19. $-54 \div -6$ = _____

20. $(-35)(16)$ = _____

21. $10 - 14 + -8$ = _____

22. $-4 - -4 + 8 - 8$ = _____

23. $-1 + -1 - -1 + 1 - -1$ = _____

24. $(-24)(36)(2)$ = _____

25. $(-3)(-3)(-3)(-3)(-3)$ = _____

26. $(-15 \div 3) + 14$ = _____

27. $-6 + (13 \bullet 0)$ = _____

28. $(-64 \div 2) \div -2$ = _____

29. $(-10 + -5)(-2)$ = _____

30. $(-12 - 18) \div -15$ = _____

31. $(163) + (-163)$ = _____

32. $(-5 - -6) \bullet -87$ = _____

33. $(42 \div -7) - 6$ = _____

34. $(-8)(-8)(-8)(-8)$ = _____

35. $15 + -6 - 13 + 5$ = _____

36. $(537)(16 + -16)$ = _____

37. $-717 \bullet \dfrac{1}{-717}$ = _____

38. $9(-9) \times 10$ = _____

39. $\dfrac{5(12 - 2)}{-25}$ = _____

40. $((-17 - 7) + (8 \bullet 3))(-57)$ = _____

Various Number Problems

OBJECTIVE: To practice estimating, patterns, computation, etc. by asking questions

A. Example

The Question: How long will it take to count to one million (counting one number per second)?

Think About: The obvious answer is one million seconds! But ask the students to give the answer in days, hours, minutes and seconds.

It is important to have students GUESS before computing.

The Solution: __11__ days, __13__ hours, __46__ minutes, __40__ seconds

There are 86,400 seconds in one day (24 h x 60 min x 60 sec).

1,000,000 ÷ 86,400 = 11.574…   so 11 days

remaining decimal x 24 = 13.7777…   so 13 hours

remaining decimal x 60 = 46.66666…   so 46 minutes

remaining decimal x 60 = 39.999…   so 40 seconds

To check (should add up to 1,000,000 seconds)

40   +   46 x 60   +   13 x 3,600   +   11 x 86,000   = 1,000,000
(seconds)   (minutes)   (hours)   (days)

B. Other Questions to Ask

(Answers will vary.) *Discuss these before computing!

...SO, LIKE, HOW MUCH WOOD COULD, LIKE, A WOODCHUCK YOU KNOW, LIKE CHUCK IF A WOODCHUCK COULD, LIKE, YOU KNOW, CHUCK, LIKE, WOOD?

1.   One million pennies are to be piled directly on top of each other. How high will the pile reach? to the ceiling? to the top of the school? to the top of the Empire State Building?

2.   One million $1 bills are placed end to end on the ground. How far will they reach? across the school gym? across the school parking lot? across the state? across the U.S?

3.   If you were to clap hands, and then clap again two minutes later, and again four minutes later and again eight minutes later and continue doubling the number of minutes between claps, how many times will you clap in one day? one week? one month? one year?

Numbers

Evaluating Expressions With Integers

Name _____

OBJECTIVE: To use rules for basic operations of integers to solve the puzzle below

Fill in the crossnumber puzzle by evaluating the expressions using the given information.

Given: A = -3, B = 4, C = -5, D = -4

Across

1. 3D
3. 9BD
6. BC + A
8. 2A + 4B
9. 5CD + B
10. 7B – D
11. 5AD + B
12. 4CD + 4A
13. 6AB
15. 2A + 3C + 4D
17. 2AC – A
19. 6C + 4A
21. 8AD + A + D
22. 9AB + C
25. 3B + 3D – 8A
26. 2CD – C
27. 4AC + 4AD
28. A – 3BC + D

Down

1. 7AB + 8D
2. 6B – 9BC
3. A + 2D
4. 7B + AD
5. 3CD – 4B
6. 6AB + 5BC + 4BD
7. 5ABC + 7B
13. A + D
14. 2A + 2B
15. A + B + D
16. AC + 2D
17. 7AD + 8AC + 9CD
18. 4BCD + 5AC
19. 7ACD + C
20. 9AC + 9AD
22. A + 2D
23. 6AC + 4BC
24. ACD + BCD – 6A

What's the Number?

Name _____

OBJECTIVE: To use patterns and problem-solving skills to answer the bogglers below

1. How many brothers and sisters are in a family in which each boy has as many sisters as brothers but each girl has twice as many brothers as sisters?

2. Try to find the missing number by discovering the pattern:

$$1 \sim 3 = 5$$
$$6 \sim 9 = 21$$
$$8 \sim 2 = 18$$
$$11 \sim 20 = ?$$

3. Using the numbers 0, 4, 8 and 12, complete the table so that each vertical, horizontal and diagonal line adds up to 24. (Use each number more than once.)

0		12	0
4			
			12

4. How many triangles can you find in each figure?

A.

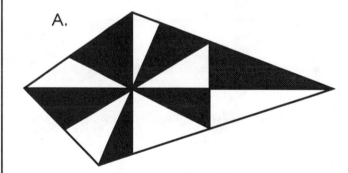

B.

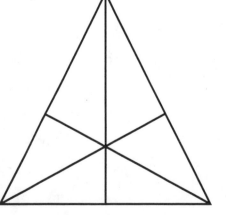

5. How many regular hexagons can you find in this figure?

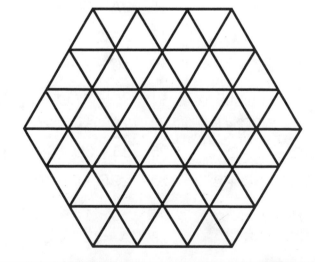

Number Patterns...Fibonacci Sequence

OBJECTIVE: To learn to discuss patterns particularly Fibonacci Sequences

To begin, ask a student to write any two numbers on the chalkboard or overhead projector (i.e. 4 and 9). Then, tell the student to find the next number in the pattern. He/she can do this by adding the first two numbers together (13). The student can continue to find other numbers in the pattern by repeating this process.

A.		B.	
1.	4	1.	a
2.	9	2.	b
3.	13	3.	$a + b$
4.	22	4.	$a + 2b$
5.	35	5.	$2a + 3b$
6.	57	6.	$3a + 5b$
7.	92	7.	$5a + 8b$
8.	149	8.	$8a + 13b$
9.	241	9.	$13a + 21b$
10.	390	10.	$21b + 34b$
	1012		$55a + 88b$

When the students reach the seventh term (92), multiply this number by 11 mentally and write that number at the bottom of the pattern. The students, in the meantime, are still calculating the eighth, ninth and tenth terms in the pattern. When they finish, ask the students to add the ten terms and write the sum at the bottom of the pattern. They will come up with the same number that you did before they even finished finding the numbers in the pattern.

At this point in the activity, the board will look like the half labeled A above. Let the students guess how you knew the answer before they finished. Allow them time to discover this. Then, give the hint to let the first number equal a, the second number equal b and complete the pattern using these variables and find the sum.

At this point, the board should look like A and B above. Again, give the students time to figure out how after the seventh number, you were able to find the sum of the ten numbers in the pattern. If they still don't see the pattern, have them multiply the seventh term by 11. Ask students why they multiplied by 11. $(5a + 8b)11 = 55a + 88b$ is the pattern for the sum of the first ten terms found by multiplying the seventh term by 11. Have students then create one of their own and verify that it works. Have them do this "trick" to friends, parents, etc.

I JUSTA LOVE FIBONACCI WITH PESTO SAUCE & A NICE GREEN SALAD... MAMA MIA!

15

Number Patterns...The School Store

Name _____

OBJECTIVE: To apply basic operations and problem-solving skills to work with the pattern in "everyday business"

A. Complete the School Store Quantity Pricing Chart

item	1	2	3	4	5	6	7	8	9	10
eraser							28¢			
pencil				24¢						
compass	25¢									
ruler			108¢							

B. Find the possible combinations for purchasing the items listed below.

1. Bill has exactly 48¢ to spend for erasers and pencils. Find the number of items he can buy.

   _6_ erasers, ____ pencils   ____ erasers, ____ pencils

   ____ erasers, _6_ pencils   ____ erasers, ____ pencils

   _0_ erasers, ____ pencils   ____ erasers, ____ pencils

   ____ erasers, _2_ pencils   ____ erasers, ____ pencils

2. Sue has $1.44 to spend for erasers, pencils and rulers. Find the number of items she can buy.

   ____ erasers, ____ pencils, _2_ rulers   ____ erasers, ____ pencils, ____ rulers

   ____ erasers, _6_ pencils, ____ rulers   ____ erasers, ____ pencils, ____ rulers

   ____ erasers, ____ pencils, _1_ ruler   ____ erasers, ____ pencils, ____ rulers

   _12_ erasers, ____ pencils, ____ rulers   ____ erasers, ____ pencils, ____ rulers

C. For each purchase, buy as many items as possible with $1.00. Fill in the missing number of items for each purchase and write what the change will be.

	1st purchase	2nd purchase	3rd purchase	4th purchase	5th purchase
pencils	3		2	2	12
erasers	5	6		1	1
rulers		1	1		
amount of change					

Number Puzzlers I

Numbers

Name _____

OBJECTIVE: To combine basic number principles with problem-solving skills on the "puzzlers" below

1. Put the numbers 1-7 in the seven circles so that the numbers in each group of three circles connected with a straight line add up to 12. Use each number only once.

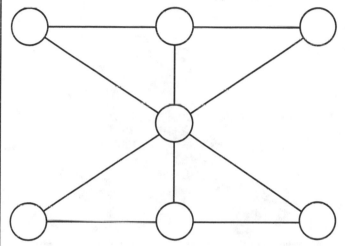

2. Draw two straight lines across the clock to divide it into three parts whose numbers within add up to 26.

3. An odd number is greater than 7 x 3 and less than 9 x 4. Find the number if the sum of its digits is 11.

4. A clock strikes the number of hours each hour. How many times will the clock strike in a 24-hour day?

5. Arrange the numbers 1-8 in the eight circles so that no two consecutive integers are in circles that are connected by line segments. Use each number only once.

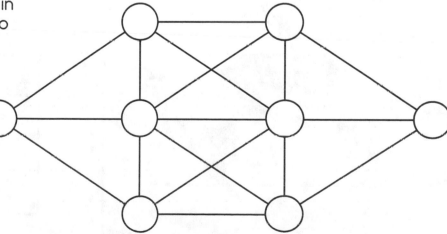

Number Puzzlers II

Name _____

OBJECTIVE: To combine basic number principles with problem-solving skills on the "puzzlers" below

1. Fill in the empty triangles using the numbers 4-9 so that the sum along each side of the large triangle equals 17. Each number may only be used once.

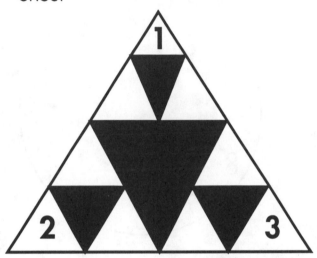

2. Fill in the empty triangles using the numbers 1-6 so that the sum along each side of the large triangle equals 23. Each number may only be used once.

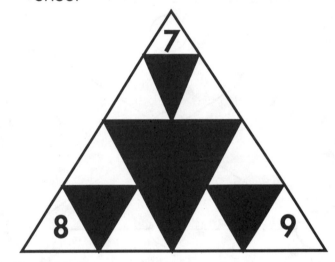

3. Make your own triangle problem. Write the rules and numbers to use. (Try it on a friend.)

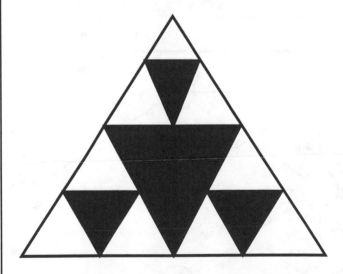

4. Put the numbers 1-12 in the twelve boxes below so that the sum of each side is 26. Each number may only be used once.

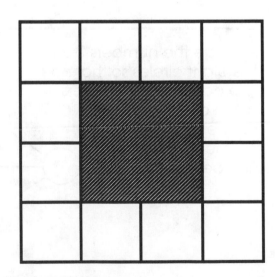

18

Numbers

The "Ultimate Square Puzzler"

Name _____

OBJECTIVE: To apply various problem-solving skills including elimination, logic patterns, basic number principles and organization in the challenging puzzle below

In the 16 squares below, place the numbers 1-8 (use each twice) using the given clues.

Clues

1. C-II contains one of the 8's.
2. Column D contains at least two odd digits.
3. Six is the largest digit in column A.
4. C-IV contains an odd number one less than its immediate left-hand neighbor.
5. No two identical digits are in adjacent squares (vertically, horizontally or diagonally).
6. A-III is twice A-II.

7. Nowhere does a 3 appear immediately below a 2.
8. Row I contains no ones.
9. Row IV totals 20, row III doesn't total 12.
10. The sum of the digits in the four corner squares, which are all different, is 12, though none of them is a 3.
11. The two 7's are in different columns and neither is in row II.
12. B-IV – B-I = C-III; D-I ≤ A-I

	A	**B**	**C**	**D**
I				
II				
III				
IV				

19

Just for Fun! (A)

Name _____

OBJECTIVE: To use various problem-solving skills to solve the puzzles below

1. Place the numbers 1-8 in the boxes so that each number is not connected to a consecutive number (not one greater or one less). Each number may only be used once.

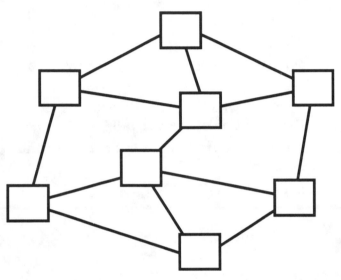

2. Using the numbers 1-9, place each number in a circle to create a sum of 20 along each side of the triangle. Each number may only be used once.

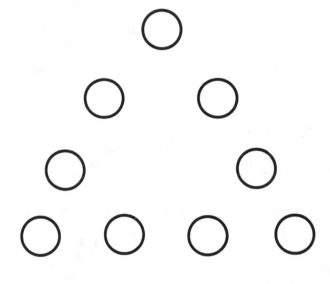

3. Using the numbers 2-10, place each number in a square to create a sum of 18 for each row, column and diagonal. Each number may only be used once.

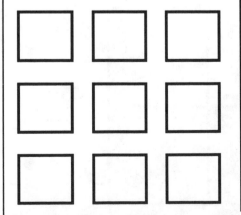

4. Arrange the numbers 1-8 in the figure shown so that no two consecutive numbers touch at a side or on a corner. Each number may only be used once.

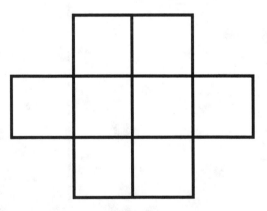

5. Arrange the nine dots in such a way that there are 8 lines with 3 dots in each line.

Numbers, Numbers, Numbers

Name _____

OBJECTIVE: To use various problem-solving skills to solve the puzzles below

1. Place the numbers 1-13 in the circles so that the sum along any line is 21. Each number may be used only once.

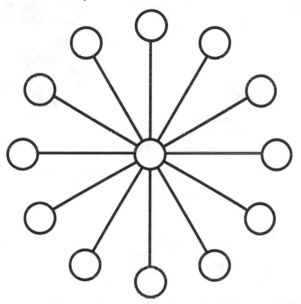

2. Complete the table and find the pattern.

Series	(N) # of Addends	(S) Sum
1	1	1
1 + 3	2	4
1 + 3 + 5		
1 + 3 + 5 + 7		
1 + 3 + 5 + 7 + 9		
1 + 3 + 5 + 7 + 9 + 11		

Pattern = _____

3. A stairway has ten steps. Each step is one foot wide and one foot high. An ant starts at the bottom of the first step and travels straight up the stairway. How far (how many feet) had the ant traveled when it reached the top of the last step? Hint: Draw a picture.

4. Place the numbers 1-11 in the circles so that the sum along any line is 18. Each number may be used only once. Hint: The number 6 has been placed for you.

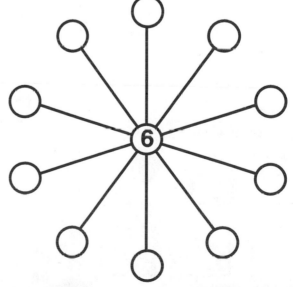

Equation-Solving "Flow Chart"

OBJECTIVE: To follow a flow chart to recognize the order and patterns of equation solving

Give students a copy of the flow chart below to use as a tool to "summarize" the equation-solving process. It can be given at any time during the learning sequence.

JUST FOR FUN:

Relate equation solving to cleaning the dishes and putting them into the dishwasher. Tell students that the pieces of the equation are like the items eaten for dinner; the variable is like the plate. If I ate pork chops, mashed potatoes, gravy, peas and applesauce for dinner, I want to "clean off my plate" before I put it in the dishwasher. So first, I quickly clear off the plate, silverware and napkin from the table (Steps 1, 2 and 3). Then, I tip the plate and all the "stuff" not stuck to the plate (peas, bones, etc.) falls into the trash can (Step 4). Lastly, I take the brush and brush off the "stuff" stuck to the plate (mashed potatoes, gravy, etc.) in order to get the plate "clean" (Step 5). Sounds silly, but you'll be surprised at how your students really remember the idea!

- -

Equation-Solving "Flow Chart"

Name _____

Solve. Show the complete step and the step number from the flow chart.

1. $x + 3 = -5$

2. $2x = 10$

3. $2x + 4 = 18$

4. $2(x - 3) = 24$

5. $7 = 6x + 19$

6. $\frac{2}{3}x + 5 = 23$

7. $-3x + 6(x - 4) = 9$

8. $3(2x + 12) = -15$

1. Is it a subtraction problem?
  (no)   (yes)
               Change it to an addition sentence.
2. Are there grouping symbols?
  (no)   (yes)
               Distribute.
3. Are there variables on the right side?
  (no)   (yes)
               Move them to the left side.
combine/simplify left side
4. Is there a number *not* attached to the variable?
  (no)   (yes)
               Move it to the right side (combine).
5. Is there a number attached to the variable?
  (no)   (yes)

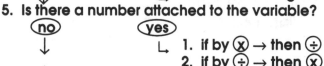

             1. if by $\times$ → then $\div$
             2. if by $\div$ → then $\times$
             3. if a fraction → then use reciprocal

variable = #
              variable = #

Applications of Equations— Numbers

Name _____

OBJECTIVES: To use various methods of problem solving to answer the number word problems below

1. One number is three less than the other. Their sum is 21. Find the numbers.

2. One number is five times another. The sum of the numbers is 108. Find the numbers.

3. The second of two numbers is four times the first. Their sum is 45. Find the numbers.

4. The sum of two numbers is 31. The first is five less than the second. Find the numbers.

Example

One number is five more than the second. Find the numbers if their sum is 115.

1.	Define variables.	let x = 2nd number
		$x + 5$ = 1st number
2.	Write equation.	$x + (x + 5) = 115$
3.	Solve and check.	$2x + 5 = 115$

$$2x + 5 + \text{-}5 = 115 + \text{-}5$$
$$\frac{2x}{2} = \frac{110}{2}$$
$$x = 55$$
$$x + 5 = 60$$
$$55 + 600 = 115$$

---

5. The second of two numbers is one more than twice the first. Their sum is 25. Find the numbers.

6. The first of two numbers is seven less than five times the second. Their sum is 113. Find the numbers.

7. The sum of three numbers is 45. The first number is four times the second, while the third number is nine more than the second. Find the numbers.

8. The sum of three numbers is 49. The second number is twice the first, and the third is one less than the second. Find the numbers.

9. The first of two numbers is nine more than the second. Three times the first is equal to seven more than five times the second. Find the numbers.

10. The greater of two numbers is five more than the smaller. If the smaller number is added to twice the greater number, the result is 22. Find the numbers.

11. The second of two numbers is six less than the first. Twice the sum of the first number and one is the same as nine times the second number. Find the numbers.

23

Applications of Equations— Measurement

Equations

Name _____

OBJECTIVES: To use various methods of problem solving to answer the measurement word problems below

---

Example

The length of a rectangle is seven times its width. The perimeter of the rectangle is 64 cm. Find the dimensions of the rectangle.

1. Draw and label figure.

   7x

   [rectangle] x

2. Define variables.

   let x = width
   x + 5 = length

3. State general formula, then specific equation.

   $P = 2(w) + 2(l)$
   $64 = 2(x) + 2(7x)$

4. Solve and check.

   $2x + 14x = 64$
   $\dfrac{16x}{16} = \dfrac{64}{16}$

   x = 4 = width
   7x = 28 = length

---

1. The length of a rectangle is 7 cm greater than the width. Find the length and the width if the perimeter is 54 cm.

2. The length of a rectangle is 5 cm more than twice the width. The perimeter is 82 cm. Find the dimensions of the rectangle.

3. The perimeter of a triangle is 26 cm. Side a of the triangle is 3 cm longer than side b. Side c is 1 cm shorter than twice side b. Find the length of each side of the triangle.

4. Each of the equal sides of an isosceles triangle is 2 inches more than three times the third side. The perimeter of the triangle is 32 inches. Find the length of each side.

5. The perimeter of a rectangle is 400 m. The length is 15 meters less than four times the width. Find the dimensions of the rectangle.

6. A triangular course for a motorcycle race is marked off by trees. The first leg of the course is 250 m longer than the second. The third leg is 100 m shorter than the first. The total length of the course is 2500 m. Find the length of each of the three legs of the course.

Equation Wrap Up

Name _____

OBJECTIVES: To practice different levels of equation solving with real numbers in the fun puzzle below

Fill in the crossnumber puzzle by solving the equations below. The decimal points have been placed in the puzzle for you.

IT'S AS EASY AS a÷b=c!

Across

1. $x + 14 = 49$

2. $4410 = 15y$

5. $a - (-328) = 930$

6. $\frac{2}{3} x = 40$

7. $c + 9.8 = 33.2$

9. $\frac{3}{100} x = \frac{72}{1000}$

11. $x^2 = 324$

Down

1. $x + {-98} = 258$

3. $\frac{1}{4} a = 105$

4. $y - 296.75 = 25.25$

6. $\frac{x}{\frac{4}{5}} = 80$

8. $x + {-2.4} = 0.68$

9. $\frac{a}{3} = 0.9$

10. $3x + 12 = 129$

Equation Fun

Equations

Name _____

OBJECTIVE: To use all basic equation-solving skills and factoring to solve this puzzle

Fill in this crossnumber puzzle by solving the equations below. Hint: Negative signs take up their own square.

Across

1. $\dfrac{x}{6} - \dfrac{x}{4} = -1$

3. $\dfrac{2}{5} = \dfrac{4}{y-4}$

4. $\dfrac{4}{12} = \dfrac{5}{a}$

5. $c = \sqrt{100}$

8. $x^2 - 12x + 36 = 0$

9. $3 = \dfrac{2+x}{6}$

10. $\dfrac{7}{x-5} = \dfrac{9}{x-3}$

11. $\dfrac{4}{x} = \dfrac{7}{x-6}$

12. $\dfrac{a}{28} = \dfrac{1}{4}$

16. $\dfrac{3y}{8} - \dfrac{1}{4} = \dfrac{y}{3} - \dfrac{11}{24}$

Down

2. $\dfrac{2}{x-7} = \dfrac{3}{x}$

5. $\dfrac{1}{2} = \dfrac{50}{a}$

6. $\dfrac{2c}{3} + \dfrac{3c}{4} = 51$

7. $\dfrac{3a}{4} - 12 = \dfrac{3(a-12)}{5}$

10. $\dfrac{2}{5} = \dfrac{x}{45}$

13. $\dfrac{6}{x-2} = \dfrac{5}{x-3}$

14. $\dfrac{y}{12} = \dfrac{5}{4}$

IS THIS FUN? ARE WE HAVING FUN NOW?

Logical Answers to Crazy Questions

OBJECTIVE: To test logic skills with the questions below

1. "Could you fit a million tennis balls in your classroom?"

   Idea:
   Have students think of ways to get a realistic answer (besides filling the room with tennis balls!).

   Try this:
   1. Bring in a shoebox (or other medium-sized box) and fill it with tennis balls. Count the number of balls in the box.
   2. Find the volume of the box.
   3. Find the volume of the classroom.
   4. Compare the two volumes and determine the number of balls needed to fill the room based on the number of balls that filled the box.

   Hints:
   Put groups of students in charge of the first three activities. Then, have each group report its information to the class. Have each student find the solution to the problem (#4 activity). Discuss students' answer(s) as a whole class. Ask the students other situations where this kind of logical process would be beneficial for problem-solving.

2. "When does 2 =1?" or "What's the big deal about dividing by zero?"

   Try this:
   Without giving the titles above, tell your students that a friend came up with a proof to show you that 2 =1. Tell students that you know it's not possible and you need help finding the "problem" with your friend's proof. Write out the proof (below) on the board. Give your students plenty of time to come up with possibilities. Discuss with the students their thoughts about this process.

   Let $a = b$.
   Then, $a \bullet a = a \bullet b$, i.e. $a^2 = ab$
   By subtracting on both sides
   $\quad a^2 - b^2 = ab - b^2$
   By factoring $(a + b)(a - b) = b(a - b)$
   By division $a + b = b$
   Therefore, $b + b = b$ (Since $a = b$)
   Finally, $2b = b$, and $2 = 1$.

   Also, you may want to point out that since division and multiplication are inverses, we know that $^6/_3 = 2$ because $2 \bullet 3 = 6$. This is helpful in understanding why $^0/_3 = 0$ (because $0 \bullet 3 = 0$) and why $^3/_0$ = undefined (because no number times zero will equal 3 or any number). Thus, stress why dividing by zero is not allowed.

27

Equations

Think About This!

Name _____

OBJECTIVES: To use various problem-solving skills to answer the questions below

1. The following answers were given by four students on a recent math quiz. No two questions have the same answer. Three students have exactly two answers correct. One student has all four wrong. What are the correct answers to this quiz? Discuss how you arrived at your answer.

Question #	Student A	Student B	Student C	Student D
1	a	d	a	b
2	c	a	b	c
3	d	c	d	a
4	b	b	c	d

2. A party was thrown for a group of scholar athletes. From the information given, determine how many athletes were at the party.

1. Ten were on the volleyball team, 9 were on the track team and 10 were on the tennis team.
2. Three of the track team members were on the volleyball team.
3. Four of the volleyball team members were on the tennis team.
4. Three of the tennis team members were on the track team.
5. No one was on more than two teams.

3. At a picnic, children get to pick from a prize box in the following way. One disc is drawn at a time from the box that contains ten red discs, ten blue discs and ten white discs. The drawing ends when three discs of the same color are drawn. If the red discs represent 5 points, the blue discs 10 points, and the white discs 20 points, what is the most points that can be won given these rules?

Factoring $x^2 + bx + c$

Name _____

OBJECTIVE: To use all basic equation-solving skills and factoring to solve this puzzle

Fill in the crossnumber puzzle by solving the equations below. One down and one across has been done as an example.

Across

1. $x^2 + 16x + 48$
2. $x^2 + 8x + 16$
3. $x^2 - 2x - 24$
5. $x^2 - 25$
6. $(\quad)^2 = x^2 - 18x + 81$
7. $x^2 - 6x + 8$
9. $x^2 - 4x - 32$
10. $x^2 + 20x + 100$
11. $x^2 + 12x + 20$
12. $x^2 - 9x + 18$
13. $x^2 - 10x + 24$
14. $x^2 + 8x + 12$
16. $(\quad)^2 = x^2 + 24x + 144$
17. $x^2 + 6x + 9$
19. $x^2 + 4x - 96$
20. $x^2 - 49$
21. $x^2 - 4x - 45$

Down

1. $x^2 - 2x - 24$
2. $x^2 + 9x + 20$
3. $x^2 - 8x + 12$
4. $x^2 - 16$
6. $x^2 + 5x - 36$
8. $x^2 + 13x + 30$
9. $x^2 - 6x - 16$
11. $x^2 + 4x - 60$
12. $x^2 - x - 30$
13. $x^2 + 8x - 48$
14. $x^2 - 2x - 48$
15. $x^2 + 14x + 24$
17. $x^2 + 10x + 21$
18. $x^2 - 15x + 54$

Factoring $ax^2 + bx + c$

Name _____

OBJECTIVES: To use all basic equation-solving skills and factoring to solve this puzzle

Fill in the crossnumber puzzle by solving the equations below. One down and one across has been done as an example.

1 $(2x-3)$	$(2x+1)$		2			3	4
$(3x+2)$		5			6	7	
	8			9			
10			11			12	
		13					
14	15	16		17			18
19			20			21	

Across

1. $4x^2 - 4x - 3$
2. $2x^2 + 9x + 4$
3. $6x^2 - 11x + 4$
5. $3x^2 - 7x - 6$
6. $4x^2 + 4x + 1 = (\ \ )^2$
7. $4x^2 - 9$
9. $9x^2 + 9x - 4$
10. $6x^2 + x - 1$
11. $4x^2 + 16x + 15$
12. $4x^2 + 13x + 3$
13. $9x^2 - 4$
14. $6x^2 - 7x - 20$
16. $9x^2 + 12x + 4 = (\ \ )^2$
17. $4x^2 - 15x - 4$
19. $6x^2 - 17x + 5$
20. $6x^2 + 5x - 6$
21. $4x^2 - 9$

Down

1. $6x^2 - 5x - 6$
2. $3x^2 + 14x + 8$
3. $6x^2 + x - 12$
4. $4x^2 - 8x + 3$
6. $6x^2 - 11x + 4$
8. $6x^2 + 11x + 4$
9. $6x^2 + 13x - 5$
11. $6x^2 + 13x + 6$
12. $8x^2 + 22x + 5$
13. $9x^2 - 4$
14. $6x^2 - 7x - 20$
15. $6x^2 - 17x + 5$
17. $8x^2 + 14x + 3$
18. $6x^2 + 17x + 12$

Consecutive Numbers Made Easy!

Name _____

OBJECTIVE: To gain a better grasp of word problems and their "mathematical" meaning by following the steps and practicing the problems

Example	The sum of two consecutive odd integers is 28. Find the numbers.	
Step	**Process**	**Concept**
1. Define variables.	let x = 1st odd number x + 2 = 2nd odd number	3 , 5 , 7 ↓ ↓ ↓ x x + 2 x + 4 (3) (3 + 2) (3 + 4)
2. Set up equation.	x + (x + 2) = 28	Reread problem replacing variables and symbols for words. "The sum of x and x + 2 equals 28."
3. Solve.	2x + 2 = 28 2x = 26 x = 13	Follow Equation-Solving Flow Chart on page 22.
4. Answer problem.	x = 13 13 + 15 = 28 x + 2 = 15 13 and 15 are the consecutive odd numbers.	Plug into definition of variables (Step 1). x = 13 (From solve step.) x + 2 = 13 + 2 = 15

Solve.

1. The sum of two consecutive even integers is 46. Find the numbers.

2. Find two consecutive odd integers whose product is 143.

3. Find two consecutive odd integers whose product is 14 more than the square of the first number.

4. Find two consecutive numbers such that the sum of their squares is 221.

5. Find two consecutive negative numbers such that the sum of their squares is 85.

6. Find three consecutive positive even integers such that the sum of their squares is 116.

Factoring Uses!

Equations

Name _____

OBJECTIVE: To improve algebraic and problem-solving skills

Example The length of a rectangle is 4 times its width. The area is 36 m². Find the dimensions.

Steps

1. Draw and label a picture.
2. Set up equation.
3. Solve.
4. Plug into definition for answer.

1.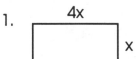

2. $(4x)(x) = 36$

3. $4x^2 = 36$
   $4x^2 - 36 = 0$
   $4(x^2 - 9) = 0$
   $4(x + 3)(x - 3) = 0$

4. $x = 3$
   $4x = 12$

---

1. Find the length of the rectangle.

   | Area is $x^2 - 5x + 6$ | $x + 2$

   ?

2. Find the length of the side of the square.

   | Area is $x^2 - 4x + 4$ | ?

3. Find the area of the rectangle.

   $(x + 6)$
   | | $(x + 3)$

4. Find the dimensions of the rectangle.

   | Area is $x^2 - 25$ |

5. A rectangular pool is 3 feet longer than it is wide. The area is 180 square feet. Find the dimensions of the pool.

6. The length of a rectangular room is one less than twice the width. The area of the room is 28 square feet. Find the dimensions of the room.

7. The width of a rectangle is 2 m less than the length. The area of the rectangle is 15 m². Find the dimensions.

8. The base of a triangle is 8 cm more than its height. If the area ($\frac{1}{2}b \cdot h$) of the triangle is 24 cm², find the base and height.

9. The area of a square is 12 more than its perimeter. Find the length of each side.

10. The perimeter of a square is 4 more than its area. Find the length of each side.

Equation-Solving Fun

Name _____

OBJECTIVE: To use the 5-step equation solving process (flow chart) to solve the puzzle below

Solve the following equations using the flow chart on page 22. Fill in the crossnumber puzzle using the answers.

Across

1. $2x - 17 = 29$
3. $3x + 16 = 73$
5. $4x + 2x = 60$
6. $\frac{1}{3}x - 3 = 6$
7. $4x + 6 = 7x$
8. $3x + 9 = 33$
9. $2x + -17 = 43$
10. $42 - x = 2x$
11. $3x - 21 = 27$
12. $2x - 41 = 35$
13. $57 = 4x - 43$
14. $\frac{x}{5} = 5$
15. $9 + 4x = 17$
16. $4x = 35 - x$
17. $32 - x = x$
18. $40 = 4x$
19. $x = 5.4 + 0.7x$
20. $3x + -45 = 57$

Down

1. $3x - 23 = 37$
2. $6 + 5x = 21$
3. $2x + x + 2x = 85$
4. $5x = 27 + 2x$
5. $8x - 6x = 36$
6. $\frac{1}{4}x + 3 = 8$
7. $2x + 7 = 55$
9. $2x = 72$
10. $6x - 61 = 47$
11. $3x - x = 30$
12. $\frac{x}{5} - 3 = 4$
13. $9x + 81 = 12x$
14. $4x - 57 = 47$
15. $x = 0.8x + 4$
17. $6x = 4x + 36$
10. $x = 0.8x + 2.8$
19. $9 = x + 2x + 6$
20. $7x = 5(x + 1) + 1$

Combination Word Problems

Name _____

OBJECTIVE: To use various methods of problem-solving skills including drawing pictures, making tables, writing equations and utilizing a graphing calculator to solve the puzzle below

Across

1. Two numbers have a difference of 8 and a sum of 22. Find the larger number.

3. Two numbers have a sum of 50 and a difference of 18. Find the smaller number.

5. Find the average of four numbers whose sum is 108.

6. The sum of two numbers is 105. The larger number is twice the smaller number. Find the smaller number.

7. Find the average of five numbers whose sum is 45.

8. A number is five times a smaller number and their sum is 144. Find the larger number.

10. A number is twice another number and their difference is 72. Find the larger number.

Combination Word Problems continued

Name _____

Across continued

11. Find the first of two consecutive numbers whose sum is 9.

12. Find the first of two odd consecutive numbers whose sum is 128.

13. Sam is 8 years older than Sue. Four years ago, Sam was twice as old as Sue. How old is Sam now?

14. Sally has 40 coins consisting of nickels and dimes equal to $3.10. How many nickels does she have?

15. The sum of the digits of a two-digit number is five. Find the number if the ten's digit is five more than the one's digit.

Down

1. Two numbers have a sum of 159 and a difference of 99. Find the larger number.

2. Two numbers have a difference of 12 and a sum of 126. Find the smaller number.

3. The sum of two numbers is 195. The larger number is twice the smaller number. Find the larger number.

4. A number is five times a smaller number. Find the larger number if their difference is 52.

8. Taylor is six years older than Jack. Two years ago, Taylor was twice as old as Jack. How old is Taylor now?

9. Find the first number of two consecutive numbers whose sum is 49.

THAR AIN'T NUTHIN' FINER THAN A PAGE FULL OF WORD PROBLEMS... 'CEPT MAYBE A PLATE FULL OF PORK 'N BEANS!

10. A number is twice another number and their sum is 207. Find the larger number.

11. Find the second of two consecutive even numbers whose sum is 798.

12. Tiffany saved $1.06 in pennies and nickels. She has 70 coins in all. How many of them are pennies?

13. The sum of the digits of a two-digit number is seven. Find the number if the one's digit is three more than the ten's digit.

Ordered Pairs

Name _____

OBJECTIVE: To gain an understanding of the coordinate system and the important relationship of the ordered pair (x, y)

I. Recall in (x, y), x indicates right or left movement from the origin and y indicates up or down movement from the origin.

State the ordered pair for each given point.

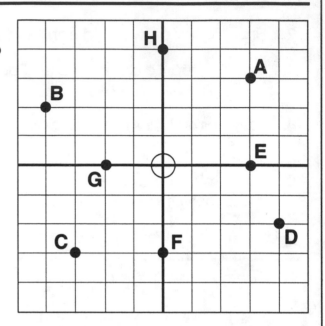

A _____   E _____

B _____   F _____

C _____   G _____

D _____   H _____

II. For this drill:

→ means move 1 to the right.

← means move 1 to the left.

↑ means move 1 up.

↓ means move 1 down.

> Example: (3,4) → = (4,4)
>
> (-2,-3) ↑ = (-2,4)
>
> (5,-8) ← = (4,-8)
>
> (3,1) ↓ = (3,0)

A. Solve.

1. (5,1) ← = _____

2. (-7, -2) ↑ = _____

3. (0,3) → = _____

4. (-2,-5) ↑ = _____

5. (0,0) ↓ = _____

6. (4,-1) → = _____

B. Fill in the table.

	Starting Point	Moves	Ending Point
ex.	(4,3)	↑ ← ← ↑	(2,5)
1.	(-3,2)	→ → → ↑ ↑ →	
2.	(6,-3)	← ↓ ← ↓ ←	
3.	(-2,-2)	↑ ↓ ↑ → → →	
4.	(7,3)	← ↓ ← ↑ → ↓	
5.	(-2,1)	→ ↑ ↑ ↑ ↑ → ↓	
6.		← ← ↓ ↓ ←	(7,7)
7.		↑ ↑ → ↑ → ↓ ↓	(-3,0)
8.		← ↓ ↓ ↑ →	(5,-2)

Box It Up (A)

Name _____

OBJECTIVE: To use shapes and visual problem-solving skills to fit pieces into puzzles

Cut out the eight shapes at the bottom of the page. These shapes were formed using one, two, three or four squares of the given 5 x 5 grid. Cover the 5 x 5 grid using all of the eight shapes. Is there more than one way it can be covered? Check with your classmates and compare answers.

The Square

The Shapes

(Shapes can be turned or flipped.)

Box It Up (B)

Name _____

OBJECTIVE: To use shapes and visual problem-solving skills to fit pieces into puzzles

The Rectangle

Cut out the nine shapes at the bottom of the page. These shapes were formed using one, two, three, four or five squares of the given 6 x 5 grid. Cover the 6 x 5 grid using all of the nine shapes. Is there more than one way it can be covered? Check with your classmates and compare answers.

The Shapes (Shapes can be turned or flipped.)

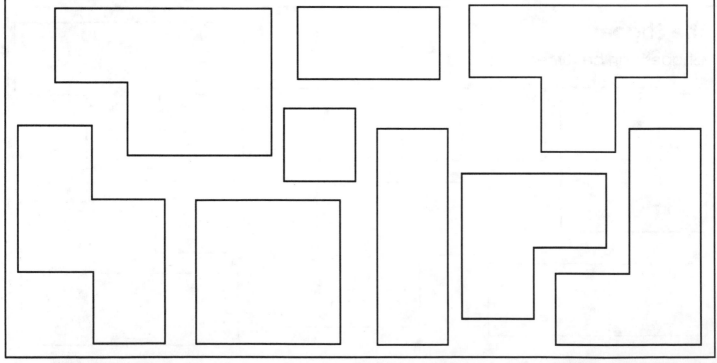

Shape Up!

OBJECTIVE: To use problem-solving skills to complete the shape problems below

Make a copy of the bottom of this page for each student. Have students complete part A visually. For part B, have students cut out each large shape and each dotted shape. Students are to use the dotted shape and a hands-on approach to solve the problem.

Shape Up!

Name _____

A—Visual Approach

Trace each figure below and finish drawing the dotted lines to divide each figure into four identical parts, each the same shape as the original picture.

1.  2. 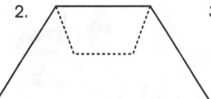 3.  4.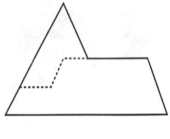

B—Hands-On Approach

Using the shapes below, divide each figure into four identical parts, each the same shape as the original figure.

1. 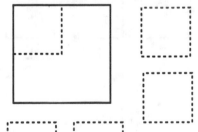   2.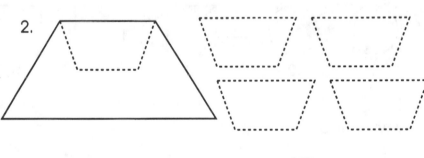

3.    4.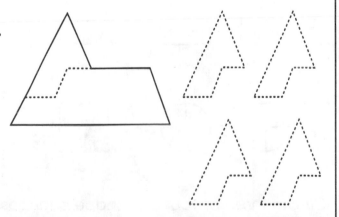

         ©Instructional Fair, Inc.

What Comes Next? (A)

Name _____

OBJECTIVES: To explore spatial relationships and to practice finding, drawing and creating shape challenges

In the problems below, shape 2 is changed in a certain way from shape 1. Shape 3 is similar to shape 1. What will the next shape look like if shape 3 is changed in the same way? Circle the correct answer.

1.  is to as is to

2. 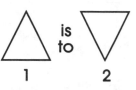 is to as is to

3. 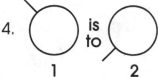 is to as 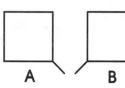 is to

4. as is to

Draw what the next shape should look like.

5. 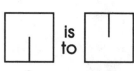 is to as is to

6. 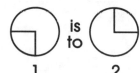 is to as is to

Create three of your own shape changes. Trade with classmates and challenge them.

What Comes Next? (B)

Name _____

OBJECTIVES: To explore spatial relationships and to practice finding, drawing and creating shape challenges

In the following problems, shape 2 is changed in a certain way from shape 1. Shape 3 is similar to shape 1. What will the next shape look like if shape 3 is changed in the same way? Circle the correct answer.

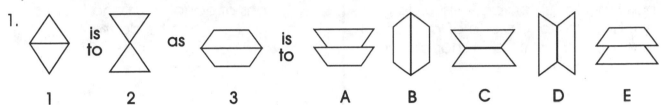

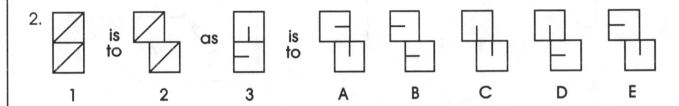

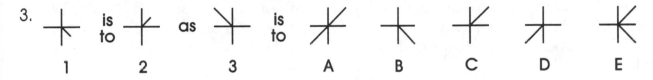

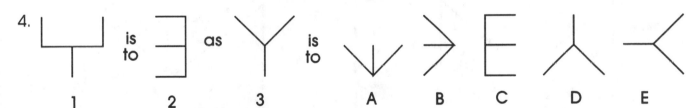

Draw what the next shape should look like.

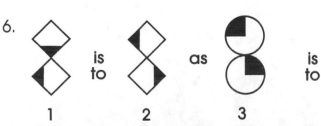

Create three of your own shape changes. Trade with classmates and challenge them.

41

Shape Splitters

Name _____

OBJECTIVES: To explore spatial relationships and to practice finding, drawing and creating shape challenges

---

1. Farmer Brown has an L-shaped piece of land with dimensions as shown. He has four daughters and wishes to give each daughter a piece of land equal in area and identical in shape. How can he do this?

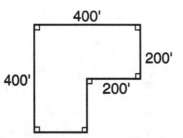

2. Farmer Green has an L-shaped piece of land and wants to create six pigpens of equal area and identical shape. How can he do this?

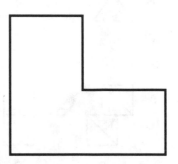

---

3. Farmer Dave needs to divide his piece of land into six equal areas and identical-shaped pens. How can he do this?

4. Farmer Sue needs to divide her piece of land into eight equal areas and identical-shaped pens. How can she do this?

---

5. How can you glue six toothpicks together to form four equilateral triangles?

Coordinate Systems/Shapes

Moving Magic (A)

Name _____

OBJECTIVES: To explore spatial relationships and to practice finding, drawing and creating shape challenges

Use real coins, toothpicks, cut-out numbers, etc. to solve the problems below.

1. Moving only three coins, make group A look like group B.

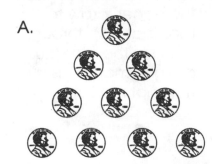
A.

B.

2. Eleven toothpicks are arranged as shown.

    a. Remove one toothpick to show four triangles.
    b. Remove two toothpicks to show four triangles.
    c. Remove two toothpicks to show three triangles.
    d. Remove three toothpicks to show three triangles.

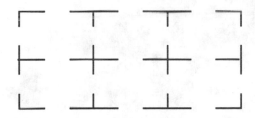

3. Move through every door in this house exactly once, without entering or exiting through the same door.

4. Place five pennies on five squares so that no two pennies are in the same row, column or diagonal.

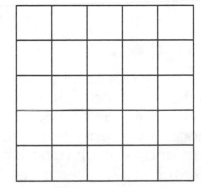

5. A coin is in a cup formed by four toothpicks as shown. Get the coin out of the cup by moving only two toothpicks. (Hint: Form a congruent cup but in a different position.)

 ©Instructional Fair, Inc.

Moving Magic (B)

Name _____

OBJECTIVES: To explore spatial relationships and to practice finding, drawing and creating shape challenges

Use real coins, toothpicks, cut-out numbers etc. to help solve the problems below.

1. Rearrange three toothpicks to form a figure that consists of three squares of the same size.

2. Rearrange three toothpicks to form a figure that consists of five squares of the same size.

3. Without lifting your pencil from the paper, draw four connected lines that pass through all nine points. (The lines must be straight, may cross a line, but may not repeat a line.)

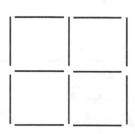

4. If Gear A turns in the direction shown by the arrow, in which direction will Gear C turn, 1 or 2?

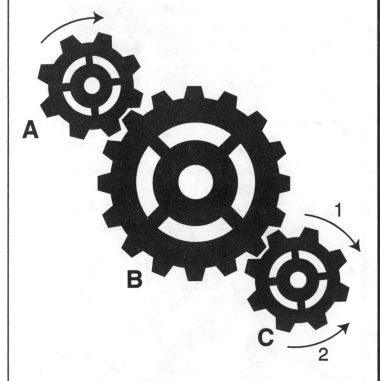

5. If Gear X has 12 cogs (teeth) and turns clockwise at 30 revolutions per minute, and Gear Y has 24 cogs, and Gear Z has 6 cogs, how fast and in which direction does Gear Z turn?

Just for Fun! (B)

Name _____

OBJECTIVE: To use counting, patterns and logic to solve brainteasers

1. Place exactly eight dots on the figure so that there are two dots in each circle and 23 dots on each line.

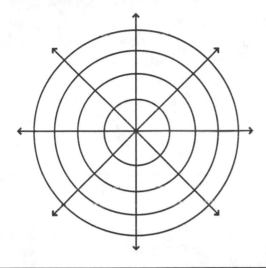

2. How many triangles are contained in this figure? (Hint: There are different sizes of triangles!)

3. Draw these figures without lifting your pencil, crossing a line or going over any line more than once.

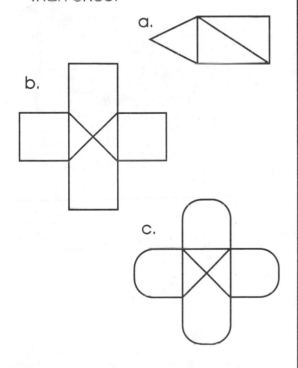

a.

b.

c.

4. A trainer has a back yard full of doghouses. He wants to put up six straight fences across the yard so that every doghouse is in a space of its own. Each doghouse should be separated by a fence. Draw lines to show where the trainer should put the fences.

Give Yourself a Hand!

OBJECTIVE: To use knowledge of area along with estimation skills to find area

YOU FOLKS HAVE BEEN GREAT... GIVE YOUR-SELVES A BIG HAND!

Have students estimate the area of their hand. Then, have them trace it on the grid on page 47 and find the area (approximately) using various methods. Have students explain the various methods and discuss which is most accurate and why, and which is the quickest and why. Discuss how various methods of estimation are valuable in different situations. Use this same technique to find the area of other items in the classroom, etc. This is a good exploratory activity! Be creative and have fun!

Other Suggestions:

Have students estimate the area of the following objects. Then, students can trace them onto the grid and find a close approximate area using rectangles. This activity should help students estimate more closely to the actual value of the area of given objects.

1. a quarter
2. a chalkboard eraser
3. a paper clip
4. a calculator
5. a stapler
6. a wallet
7. a foot
8. the base of a coffee cup
9. a dollar bill
10. a crumpled piece of paper
11. a highlighter pen
12. a keychain (with or without keys)
13. a leaf or flower
14. a rock
15. a watch
16. a pencil
17. Come up with some more items to estimate and measure.

Give Yourself a Hand!
continued

Name _____

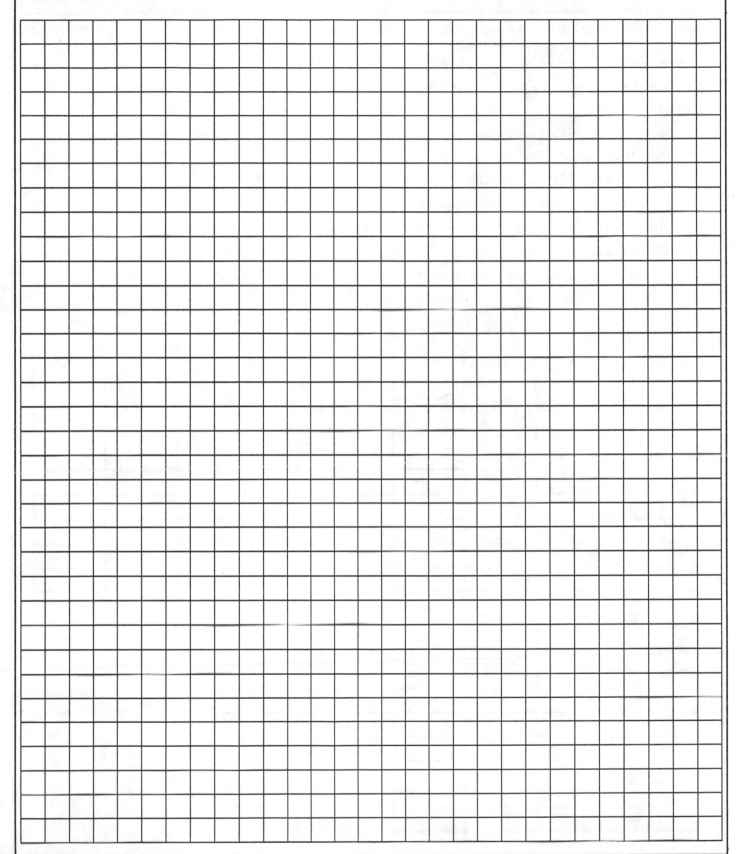

47

Logic (Survey)

Name _____

OBJECTIVE: To use matrix logic puzzles to organize thoughts and to approach problem solving in a more logical manner

Given the clues below find on which day, where and on what subject each person was interviewed.

1. Terri, who was questioned after both Pat and Sam in the week, was asked about electronics, but not at the bank.
2. Linda was interviewed at town hall.
3. Pat was interviewed two days after Sam.
4. The political questionnaire was given on Wednesday.
5. The person questioned at the bus stop was asked about food labeling.
6. Friday's interview was not about TV and did not take place in the mall.
7. Tuesday's interview took place at the train station.

	Monday	Tuesday	Wednesday	Thursday	Friday	Bank	Bus Stop	Train Station	Mall	Town Hall	Electronics	Food Labeling	Newspapers	Politics	TV
Pat															
Linda															
Terri															
Paula															
Sam															
Electronics															
Food Labeling															
Newspapers															
Politics															
TV															
Bank															
Bus Stop															
Train Station															
Mall															
Town Hall															

Company Communication

Name _____

OBJECTIVE: To use patterns and grouping to solve the friendly puzzle below

On the map of the United States below, eleven cities are marked with dots. In each city is the office of a nationwide communication company with sales representatives who work with sales representatives in another city. The people who work together must get along. The eleven sales representatives are:

Annette	Elaine	Ira
Bill	Frank	James
Carl	Gail	Kim
David	Harold	

The friends are:

Annette and Bill	Frank and Harold	Ira and Kim
Ira and James	Gail and James	Gail and Ira
David and Elaine	James and Carl	David and Ira
Annette and Gail	Kim and Elaine	Kim and David
Carl and Harold	Annette and David	

Place the eleven sales representatives in the eleven cities so that they work with their friends in the connecting offices.

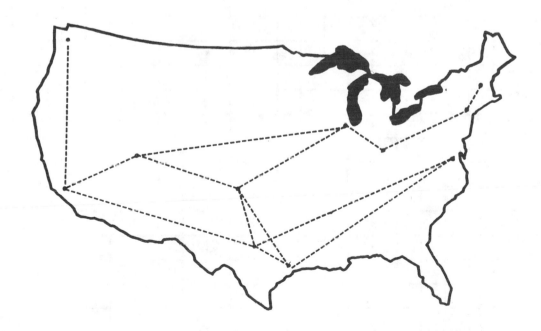

Big Screen Tic-Tac-Toe

OBJECTIVE: To use logic and problem-solving skills to try to get five marks in a row before the opponent

Make plenty of copies of the page below for students to use on lots of occasions.

Rules: One player marks X's and the other marks O's in an alternating pattern in the boxes. The winner is the first one to get five marks in a row vertically, horizontally or diagonally. (It is like tic-tac-toe, except it is played on a grid with hundreds of boxes instead of just nine.)

Gameboard:

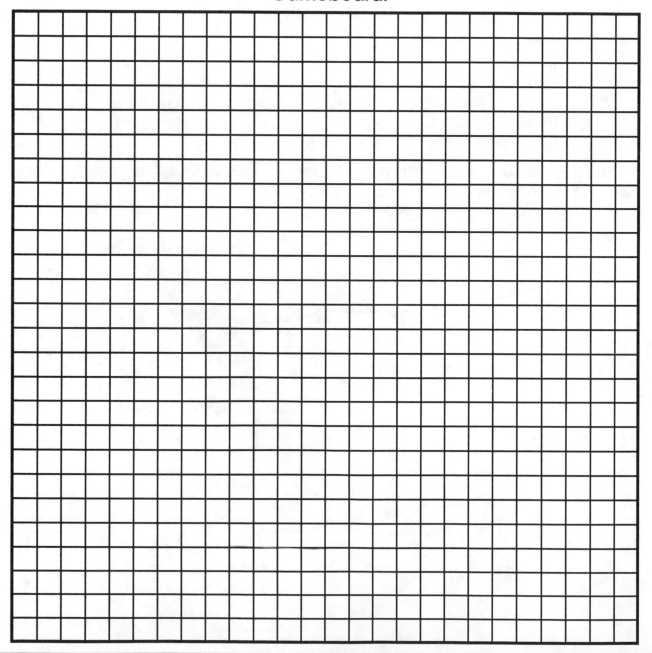

Order in the Square

OBJECTIVE: To use problem-solving skills to put the numbers below in order without lifting any pieces

Copy and cut out a classroom set. (Laminate all pieces and store each puzzle in a resealable plastic bag for easy use!)

- -

Rules: Without picking up a number square, try to move the squares (by sliding only one at a time into an open space) to put them in the shown order. Think through your moves. Race a neighbor for greater challenge.

Begin with the pieces as shown in Figure A. You have completed the puzzle successfully when your square looks like Figure B.

Figure A
Start here.

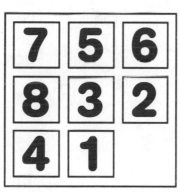

Figure B
End here.

```
1 2 3
4 5 6
7 8
```

- -

Cut out and laminate.

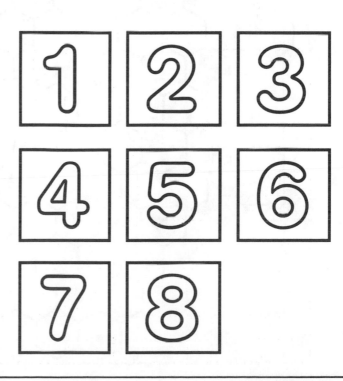

Don't Break the Chain!

OBJECTIVE: To use problem-solving skills to complete a chain from one end to the other end before the opponent

Make plenty of copies of these to use on any occasion.

Rules: One player marks X's and the other marks O's in an alternating pattern in the boxes. The winner is the first one to complete a chain from one side to the opposite side (O's top to bottom and X's side to side). The chain needs only to be connected marks, not necessarily in a straight line. See example below.

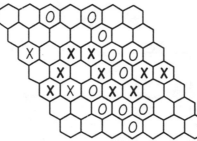

In this game, X's won because Player X got a chain of X's across the board.

Gameboard:

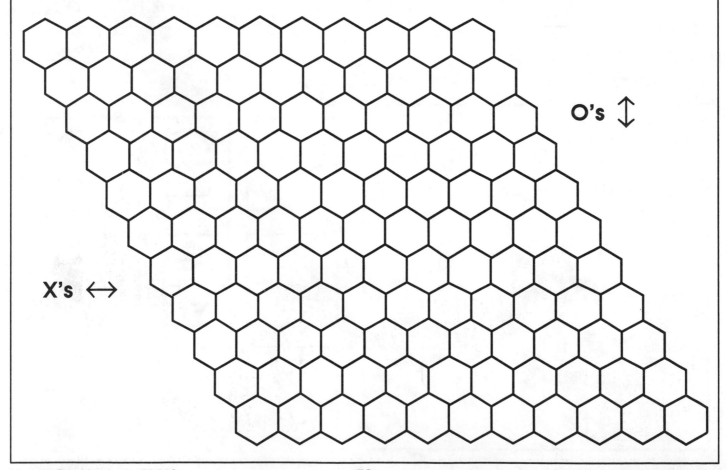

O's ↕

X's ↔

52

Tangrams

OBJECTIVE: To use tangrams to create various mathematical and non-mathematical pictures; Different patterns and visual problem solving will be explored.

The tangram is a geometric puzzle used to form various figures. This is a great way to get students working with shapes. Use the overhead tangrams to show students the tangram puzzle put together. Then, take the puzzle apart, piece by piece, and explain each

TANGRAM FOR MR. RIDER, TANGRAM FOR MR. RIDER... OH... ER, UH...SORRY, THAT'S TELEGRAM FOR MR. RIDER, TELEGRAM FOR MR. RIDER!

piece. Show students how the pieces can fit together to form other figures.

Give each student a copy of the puzzle on the bottom of page 56. Have the students cut the tangram puzzle into seven pieces on the solid lines. Using the seven pieces, have the students put them back together to make the square. Below are some activities to use with the tangrams.

1. Students can work individually to create specific pictures or to invent a few of their own.

2. Have two students "race" each other to piece together a shape or object.

3. Students can race to see how many specific shapes they can create in five minutes. (Keep track of ongoing progress.)

Enlarge the shapes below and on pages 54-56 and make a booklet. Have students flip through the booklet and try to make the figures. There are so many great ways to use tangrams. Have fun!

Tangrams

1.   2.   3.   4.

Tangrams continued

5.

6.

7.

9.

10.

11.

8.

12.

13.

14.

15.

16.

17.

18.

19.

Tangrams continued

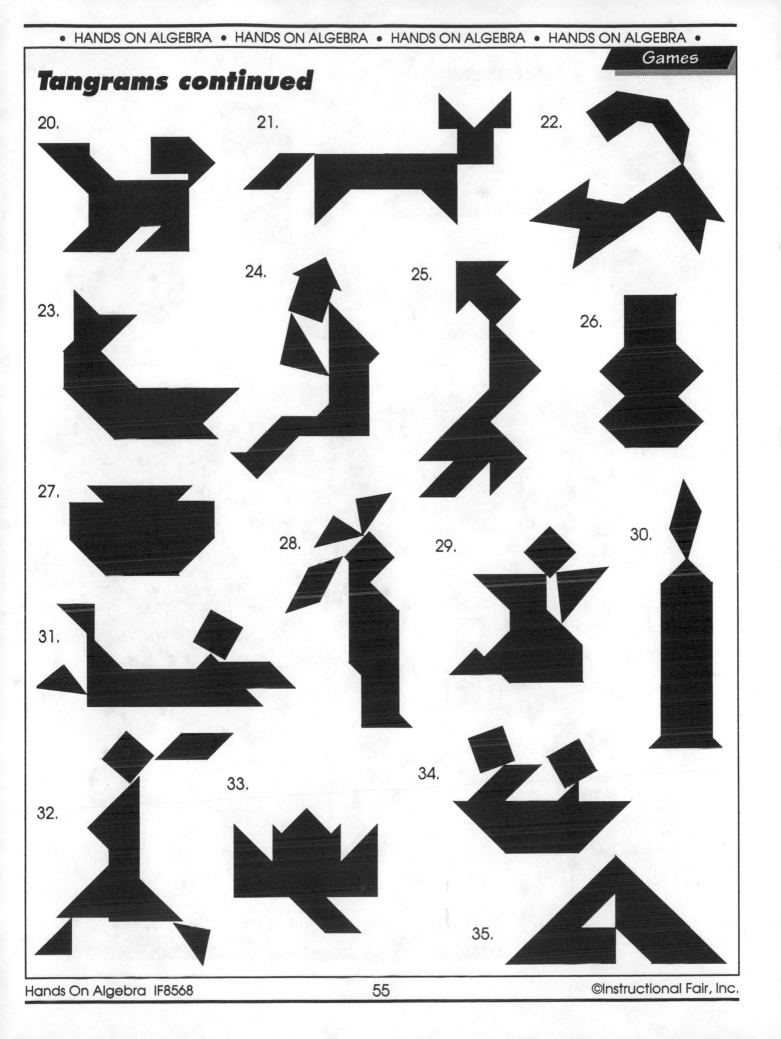

20.

21.

22.

23.

24.

25.

26.

27.

28.

29.

30.

31.

32.

33.

34.

35.

Tangrams continued

36.

37.

39.

40.

38.

Laminate
and cut out.

Trash Can Hoops

OBJECTIVES: To practice gathering, organizing and analyzing data and to learn to solve ratio and percent problems

---

For the Teacher: Have teams compete against each other to see who has the highest percent of shots made.

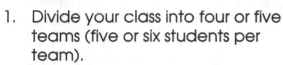

1. Divide your class into four or five teams (five or six students per team).

2. Have pre-made pieces of paper cut with the numbers 2, 4, 5 and 10 on them. Each member of each team should pick one of the numbers. This will tell each student how many shots he/she gets to take.

3. Each player should stand 10 feet away from a wastebasket and attempt to throw a crumpled paper ball into the can. He/she should shoot the number of times as directed by the number previously drawn.

4. The teams then compete to see which can score the most baskets per shot taken (the winners!).

5. Each student can keep a scorecard for his/her own team. The scorecard below can be copied for each student.

6. Teach ratio and percent problems using this as a tool to actually introduce the two concepts. Discuss other everyday situations in which these mathematical models may be used.

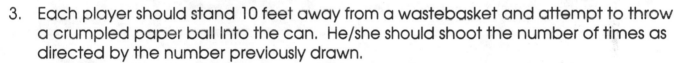

Team _____	# of shots made	# of shots taken	ratio of shots made to shots taken	ratio of shots converted to $\frac{}{100}$	% of shots made
Total					

Games

Battleship (Instructions/Example)

OBJECTIVE: To play the game of battleship while practicing ordered pairs, coordinate systems and problem-solving skills

Pair up students. Have the pairs turn their desks so that they face each other. Each student should use a book as a game holder. (Have students open the cover to create a private table.) Give each student a copy of page 59, "Battleship A." Each student has five ships—a one-man, a two-man, a three-man, a four-man and a five-man ship. Ships can be placed vertically, horizontally or diagonally as long as each "man" is on a point on the grid. Students should put their ships on the upper "My Ship" grid on the page. After both players have hidden their ships in the upper grid, the game can begin. The rules for the game need to be understood by all players before beginning.

Rules:

The youngest of the pair is Player One. To begin, Player One gets five guesses to try to find Player B's ships. After all five guesses, Player Two must tell which guesses were hits and which ship(s) was sunk. Then, Player Two gets five guesses and Player One must tell which were hit and sunk. The play continues alternating turns. The only catch is that when one player loses a ship, he/she loses a guess. (For example, If Player Two only has three ships left, he/she only gets three guesses instead of five.) A player wins when he/she sinks all five of the opponent's ships.

Tell students that an easy way to keep track of what they call is to make marks on their grids. For example, on the top grid, if the opposing player hits a ship, tell students to put an x over the dot (✗). On the lower grid, as they call out ordered pairs, they should make a dot on the points called. If the dot was a hit, have them cross it out (✗). This way, students won't call the same points over and over and waste guesses.

To give students practice using all four quadrants, give them page 60, "Battleship B."

Player One

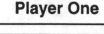

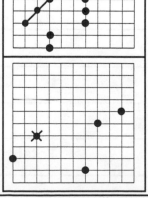

Example

1. Player One places his/her ships as shown.
2. Player One guesses (2, 4), (6, 1), (9, 6), (7, 5) and (0, 2).
3. Player Two tells him/her that (2, 4) is a hit on the two-man ship. (Player Two still has five guesses because his/her two-man ship was hit but not sunk.)

Battleship A

Name _____

My Ships

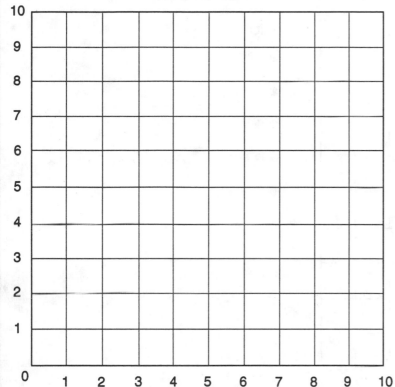

Ships:

- •
- • •
- • • •
- • • • •
- • • • • •

Enemy Ships

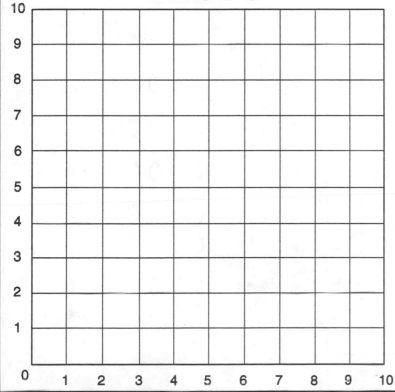

Location:

•   (   )

• •   (   ) (   )

• • •   (   ) (   ) (   )

• • • •   (   ) (   ) (   )
          (   )

• • • • •   (   ) (   ) (   )
          (   ) (   )

Battleship B

Name _____

My Ships

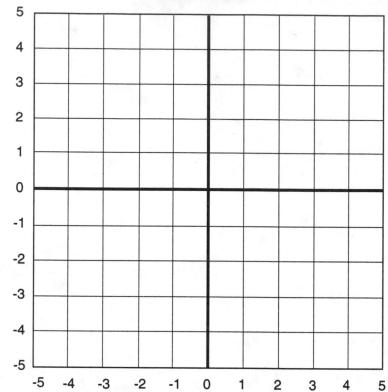

Ships:

•

••

•••

••••

•••••

Enemy Ships

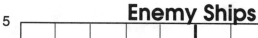

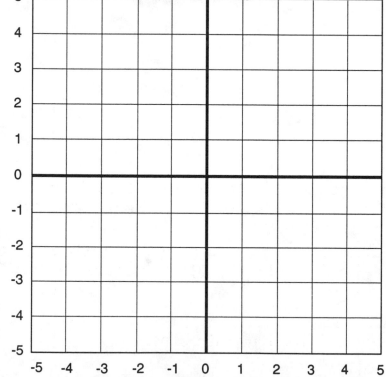

Location:

•   (   )

••   (   )(   )

•••   (   )(   )(   )

••••   (   )(   )(   )
            (   )

•••••   (   )(   )(   )
            (   )(   )

Tri-Connecting These!

OBJECTIVE: To use logic and problem-solving skills to connect game pieces

Materials:
copies of page 62 and 63; paper; pencil; large, flat playing area

Directions:
Copy the bottom of page 62 and page 63 to make one set of game pieces for 2-4 students. (Make one set for each group of students.) Laminate pages 62 and 63 and cut apart the triangles to form the game pieces. Divide your students into teams of 3-4. Give each team one set of triangle game pieces, a piece of paper, a pencil and a copy of the rules below and on page 62. You might want to go over the rules with the students before they begin playing the game. Make a sample score sheet (See below.) on the board for students to follow. Make sure each team has a large surface area (desk or floor) to play on. The game can be won by points or by time, whichever you decide. For example, at the end of the hour, the player with the highest total in each group wins. Or, the first player to reach 200 points wins. (Suggestion: Play by time the first time your class plays; then select a logical point total to play to next time.)

Rules:
1. Make a score sheet similar to the one shown.

2. Place all of the triangle game pieces, numbers down, on the playing surface and mix well.

Bill	Sue	Bob

3. Each player selects the given number of game pieces. Keep the game pieces hidden from the opponents with a book or folded piece of paper.

# of Players	# of Triangle Pieces
2	9 each
3	7 each
4	6 each

4. The player to start is the player with the triangle that has the highest total of points.

   (For example, ⬩ is the highest with 15 points.)
   That triangle is placed, numbers up, in the middle of the playing surface. That player is given the point value of the numbers on the triangle plus a 20-point bonus for starting. (Example: 5 + 5 + 5 = 15 + 20 = 35 points)

5. Moving in a counterclockwise manner, the next player tries to match any two numbers on the first triangle. If this is done, that player is given the total of numbers of his/her triangle as points. Play continues is this manner.

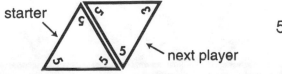

5 + 5 + 3 = 13 points

61 ©Instructional Fair, Inc.

Tri-Connecting These! continued

6. If the next player cannot match, he/she must pick from the "pool" of remaining triangles still numbers down. For each pick, 5 points will be deducted from his/her score for that play. The player must continue to pick until a match can be made. When a match is finally made, the scorekeeper must deduct the total number of points and add the points from the turn.

7. If a player matches all 3 triangles on a triangle (thus forming a hexagon) add the sum of the numbers on the triangle to the score. Plus, give that player a 50-point bonus.

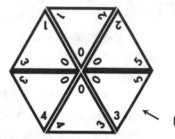

$0 + 3 + 5 = 8 + 50 = 58$ points

8. If a player matches two numbers on one triangle and the third number on another (forming a bridge), add the sum of the numbers on the triangle to the score plus give that player a 30-point bonus.

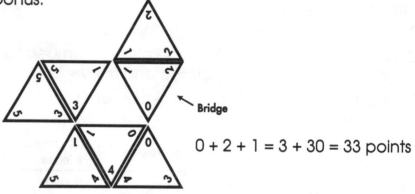

Bridge

$0 + 2 + 1 = 3 + 30 = 33$ points

9. The game is won by points or by time. Your teacher will tell you which to use.

10. If a player cannot match with any in his/her hand, and there are none left in the pool, he/she must pass. Ten points are deducted from his/her score. If all the players pass, the game is over and the player with the most points is the winner.

- -

Copy and cut out the triangle strips below and on page 63. Cut the individual triangles apart and laminate them. Store the pieces in a resealable bag.

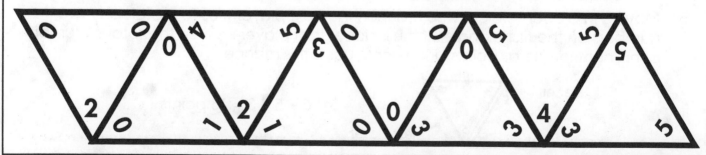

62

Tri-Connecting These! continued

Discovering Lines

OBJECTIVE: To use the worksheet below to discover slopes, intercepts and graphs of lines

Recall a few general facts about linear equations:

general form	$ax + by = c$
slope-intercept form	$y = mx + b$
point-slope form	$y - y_1 = m(x - x_1)$

$$m = \frac{y_1 - y_2}{x_1 - x_2}$$

$b = y$–intercept
(when $x = 0$)

$m = $ slope

Note:
RANGE — should be set as follows:

$x_{min} = -10$
$x_{max} = 10$
$x_{sc1} = 1$
$y_{min} = -10$
$y_{max} = 10$
$y_{sc1} = 1$
$x_{res} = 1$

Exploring Slope and y_0 (Graph one at a time, adding the next $y_\#$ as you go.)

Graph the four lines in each group. Notice what happens to the line when the coefficient of x is changed in the following ways. Describe.

1. a. $y_1 = 5x$ _____

    b. $y_2 = x$ _____

    c. $y_3 = .5x$ _____

    d. $y_4 = 5$ _____

2. a. $y_1 = 5x$ _____

    b. $y_2 = -5x$ _____

    c. $y_3 = 2x$ _____

    d. $y_4 = -2x$ _____

3. a. $y_1 = 5x + 3$ _____

    b. $y_2 = 5x - 3$ _____

    c. $y_3 = -2x + 6$ _____

    d. $y_4 = 2x - 6$ _____

Discuss (and explore further) how the coefficient of x (slope) changes the graph. Discuss positive, negative, zero and "no slope" concepts. Discuss what the x and y intercepts are and how to find them.

Matrices A (Determinants)

Name _____

OBJECTIVES: To learn how to use the matrix function on the TI-81 and to be able to solve determinants and systems of equations using matrices

Finding the Value of a Determinant

A determinant is the numerical value of a rectangular array of numbers.

Example 1	$\begin{vmatrix} 3 & 5 \\ -2 & 1 \end{vmatrix}$	=	$(3)(1) - (-2)(5)$

$$3 - -10$$
$$13$$

Example 2	$\begin{vmatrix} 2 & 6 & 1 \\ 3 & -5 & -1 \\ 4 & 2 & 2 \end{vmatrix}$	$= 2\begin{vmatrix} -5 & -1 \\ 2 & 2 \end{vmatrix} - 6\begin{vmatrix} 3 & -1 \\ 4 & 2 \end{vmatrix} + 1\begin{vmatrix} 3 & -5 \\ -4 & 2 \end{vmatrix} = -50$

To Do Example 2 Using the TI-81   (The keys in bold are the 2nd function keys.)

[ON]

[MATRX]

[▶] to Edit

[ENTER] (1: [A])

Enter the size of the matrix (row x column) by hitting **3** [ENTER] **3** [ENTER].

Enter the numbers in the matrix (by row, column) as **2** [ENTER] **6** [ENTER] **1** [ENTER] continued.

[2nd] [QUIT] (You will really be punching the [CLEAR] key.)

[MATRX]

5 (det)

[2nd] [A]

[ENTER]

Answer will show as -50.

Practice

Find the value of the following determinants using the TI-81.

1. $\begin{vmatrix} 7 & 9 \\ 3 & 6 \end{vmatrix}$

2. $\begin{vmatrix} 8 & 9 & 3 \\ 3 & 5 & 7 \\ -1 & 2 & 4 \end{vmatrix}$

3. $\begin{vmatrix} 6 & 7 & 4 \\ -2 & -4 & 3 \\ 1 & 1 & 1 \end{vmatrix}$

4. $\begin{vmatrix} 14 & 21 \\ 26 & 39 \end{vmatrix}$

5. $\begin{vmatrix} 3 & 0 & 2 \\ 0 & -1 & 5 \\ 6 & 7 & 0 \end{vmatrix}$

6. $\begin{vmatrix} 7 & 0 & 9 & 5 \\ 8 & 2 & -1 & 2 \\ -5 & 3 & 7 & 9 \\ 0 & -1 & -4 & -6 \end{vmatrix}$

Matrices B (Solving Systems of Equations)

Name _____

OBJECTIVES: To learn how to use the matrix function on the TI-81 and to be able to solve determinants and systems of equations using matrices

To Solve a System of Equations

Example	$y - 3x = 8$
	$x + y = 4$

Note:
3 equations with 3 unknowns would require a 3 x 3 ([A]) and a 3 x 1 ([C]) (3 rows, 1 column)

1. Rewrite into $-3x + y = 8$
                         $x + y = 4$

2. Enter into a 2 x 2 matrix the x and y coefficient of each equation (MATRIX [A]).

3. Enter the constants into a 2 x 1 matrix. (Use MATRIX [C] for "constants."

4. Type in [2nd] [A] [x⁻¹] [2nd] [C] [ENTER] .
   Answers will show   [-1]   meaning x = -1
                               [5]   y = 5
                               or (-1, 5)

Practice

(Hint: Where no x or y exists, place a zero as the coefficient.)

1. $-2x + y = -4$
    $5x - y = -2$

2. $x - 2y = 8$
    $2x + y = 6$

3. $-3x + 2y = -3$
    $5x - 3y = 5$

4. $2y = x - 8$
    $y - 3 = 4x$

5. $2x - y = -2$
    $-2x + 3y = 0$

6. $4x - 2y = 25$
    $x + 2y = 10$

7. $3x + 4y = 5$
    $2x + 3y = 5$

8. $3x + 2y = 5$
    $2x - y = 8$

9. $x - 2y + 3z = 2$
    $2x - 3y + x = 1$
    $3x - y + 2x = 9$

10. $x + 2y + z = 3$
     $2x - 3y + 2z = -1$
     $x - 3y + 2z = 1$

11. $2x + 3y = 4z + 5$
     $x + y + 2z = 3$
     $-x + 2y - 6z = 4$

Distance Formula

Name _____

OBJECTIVES: To use the formula below to find the distance between two points and to solve applications of distance problems

Program

To enter the distance program on the calculator, do the following steps:

[PRGM]

[▶] to Edit

[ENTER] (or [▼] to next available program)

DISTANCE

[ENTER]

[PRGM]

[▶] to I/O

5 (Clr Home)

[ENTER]

⎡ [PRGM]

  [▶] to I/O

  [ENTER] (Disp)

  [2nd] [A-LOCK] ["] X [ALPHA] 1 [2nd] [A-LOCK] ["]

  [ENTER]

  [PRGM]

  [▶] to I/O

  2 (Input) [ALPHA] A

⎣ [ENTER]

> **Program appears as:**
> **Prgm (#): DISTANCE**
> : Clr Home
> : Disp "x1"
> : Input A
> : Disp "y1"
> : Input B
> : Disp "x2"
> : Input C
> : Disp "y2"
> : Input D
> : $\sqrt{\ }\ ((A - C)^2 + (B - D)^2 \to E$
> : Disp "DISTANCE IS"
> : Disp E
> : End

Repeat the sequence in the bracket for "y1" through D in the program in the shaded box above. Then, continue with the rest of the program below and on page 68.

[2nd] [√] (([ALPHA] A − [ALPHA] C) x² + ([ALPHA] B − [ALPHA] D) x² [STO▶] E [ENTER]

[PRGM]

[▶] to I/O

[ENTER] (Disp)

[2nd] [A-LOCK] ["] DISTANCE [␣] IS [2nd] [A-LOCK] ["]

[ENTER]

[PRGM]

[▶] to I/O

[ENTER] (Disp)

Distance Formula continued

TI-81 Graphing Calculator

Name _____

ALPHA E
ENTER
PRGM
7 (End)
2nd QUIT

To view program, follow the sequence below.
(Program should appear as shown in gray box on page 67.)

   PRGM
   ▶ to Edit
   (▼ to program number) or ENTER
   ▼ along program

| **Example** | Find the distance between (2, 5) and (6, 2). |

PRGM
(▼ to program number) or ENTER
ENTER
2
ENTER
5
ENTER
6
ENTER
2
ENTER

Program appears as:
Prgm (#):
x1
?2
y1
?5
x2
?6
y2
?2
DISTANCE IS
          5

Practice

1. (9, 4) (3, -2)

2. (1, -3) (5, 2)

3. (-2, 4) (-1, 2)

4. (3, 1) (-3, 6)

5. (-2, -3) (1, 2)

Applications

(Hint: Use the Distance Formula Program along with the Pythagorean Theorem.)

Do the points (given as vertices of a triangle) form a right triangle? (4, 4) (6, 10) (10, 2)
What methods did you use to verify this? What about (-5, 7) (-2, 2) (7, 2)? or (-6, -2)
(-5, -4) (-3, 1)? or (4, 11) (10, 3) (4, 3)? Discuss.

TI-81 Graphing Calculator

Quadratic Formula

OBJECTIVES: To solve various quadratic equations and to apply problem-solving skills

After students learn the Quadratic Formula, have them program the formula below into the TI-81 and discover how easy these problems really are.

Program

Enter on calculator.

[PRGM]

[▶] to Edit

[ENTER] (or [▼] to next available program)

QUADFORM

[ENTER]

[PRGM]

[▶] to I/O

5 (Clr Home)

[ENTER]

[PRGM]

[▶] to I/O

[ENTER] (Disp)

[2nd] [A-LOCK] ["] ENTER

[⎵] A [2nd] [A-LOCK] ["]

[ENTER]

[PRGM]

[▶] to I/O

2 (Input) [ALPHA] A

[ENTER]

Repeat the sequence in the bracket for "Enter B", Input B, "Enter C" and Input C.

Enter the next lines on the program. Remember when punching in letters to hit the [ALPHA] key. Also, remember to hit the [2nd] key when you need a 2nd function key.

: $B^2 - 4 \times A \times C \to D$
: $(-) B - \sqrt{D} \to E$
: $(-) B + \sqrt{D} \to F$
: $E / (2 \times A) \to G$
: $F / (2 \times A) \to H$
: **Disp "The Values Are"**
: **Disp G**
: **Disp "And"**
: **Disp H**
: **End**

View the program after you have entered it to make sure it appears exactly as in the gray box.

Program appears as:

Prgm (#): QUADFORM
: **Clr Home**
: **Disp "Enter A"**
: **Input A**
: **Disp "Enter B"**
: **Input B**
: **Disp "Enter C"**
: **Input C**
: $B^2 - 4 * A * C \to D$
: $-B - \sqrt{D} \to E$
: $-B + \sqrt{D} \to F$
: $E / (2 * A) \to G$
: $F / (2 * A) \to H$
: **Disp "The Values Are"**
: **Disp G**
: **Disp "And"**
: **Disp H**
: **End**

Example	Try $x^2 - 5x + 6$

[PRGM] (Exec)

[ENTER] or # of program

[ENTER]

Then, key in the numbers below.

A = 1

B = -5

C = 6

Answer should be 2 and 3.

Practice

1. $x^2 - 7x + 12 = 0$

2. $x^2 - 8x - 9 = 0$

3. $x^2 = -7x - 10$

4. $2x^2 - 5x - 3 = 0$

5. $6x^2 + 7x = -2$

6. $x^2 + 2x + 1 = 0$

7. $4x^2 - 24x + 20 = 0$

8. $2x^2 + 13x = -15$

9. $2x^2 - 7x - 4 = 0$

10. $5x^2 - 42x - 27 = 0$

Area of Triangles

TI-81 Graphing Calculator

Name _____

OBJECTIVE: To use the program below to find the area of a triangle when the lengths of three sides are given

This program is basically Heron's Formula. This can be helpful in finding the area when the height is not known. Also, it is useful in combination with other programs to solve many applications.

Heron's Formula
$s = \frac{1}{2}(a + b + c)$
$k = \sqrt{s(s - a)(s - b)(s - c)}$

Program

Enter on calculator.

PRGM

▶ to Edit

ENTER (or ▼ to next available program)

TRIAREA

ENTER

PRGM

▶ to I/O

5 (Clr Home)

ENTER

PRGM

▶ to I/O

ENTER (Disp)

2nd A-LOCK " SIDE ␣ A 2nd A-LOCK "

ENTER

PRGM

▶ to I/O

2 (Input) ALPHA A

ENTER

Repeat the sequence in the bracket for B and C. Then, continue with the program.

(ALPHA A + ALPHA B + ALPHA C) ÷ 2 STO▶ S

ENTER

2nd √ (S (S – A) (S – B) (S – C)) STO▶ K

(Remember to hit ALPHA prior to each letter.)

ENTER

PRGM

▶ to I/O

ENTER (Disp)

2nd A-LOCK " AREA ␣ IS 2nd A-LOCK "

ENTER

PRGM

▶ to I/O

ENTER (Disp) ALPHA K

ENTER

PRGM

Prgm 7 (end)

View the completed program to make sure it appears as in the gray box.

Program appears as:

Prgm (#): TRIAREA
: Clr Home
: Disp "Side A"
: Input A
: Disp "Side B"
: Input B
: Disp "Side C"
: Input C
: (A + B + C) / 2 → S
: √ (s(s – a)(s – b)(s – c)) → K
: Disp "Area is"
: Disp K
: End

Practice

Find the area of the following triangles with sides of the given lengths.

1. $a = 3, b = 4, c = 5$

2. $a = 20, b = 21, c = 29$

3. $a = 4, b = 5, c = 6$

4. $a = 3, b = 5, c = 7$

Synthetic Division

OBJECTIVE: To use the program below and on page 72 to complete synthetic division problems

Program

Enter on calculator.

PRGM
▶ to Edit
ENTER (or ▼ to next available program)
SYNTH
ENTER
PRGM ▶ to I/O
5 (Clr Home)
ENTER
2nd STAT ▶ ▶ (DATA) 2 (Clr Stat)
ENTER
PRGM ▶ to I/O
ENTER (Disp)
2nd A-LOCK ⟦"⟧ **POLY ⟦␣⟧ DEGREE**
   2nd A-LOCK ⟦"⟧
ENTER
PRGM ▶ to I/O
2 (Input) ALPHA **N**
ENTER
PRGM ▶ to I/O
ENTER (Disp)
2nd A-LOCK ⟦"⟧ ⟦"⟧ ENTER
PRGM ▶ to I/O
ENTER (Disp)
2nd A-LOCK ⟦"⟧ **COEFFICIENTS**
   2nd A-LOCK ⟦"⟧
ENTER
O STO▶ **I**
ENTER
PRGM
ENTER ([b1)
1
ENTER
ALPHA **N −** ALPHA **I** STO▶ **E** ENTER
PRGM ▶ to I/O
ENTER (Disp)

ALPHA **E**
ENTER
PRGM ▶ 2 (Input)
2nd ⟦{x}⟧ ALPHA **I** ⟦+⟧ **1** ⟦)⟧
ENTER
PRGM
4 (IS>() ALPHA **I** ALPHA **,** ALPHA **N** ⟦)⟧
ENTER
PRGM
2 (Goto) **1**
ENTER
PRGM ▶ to I/O
ENTER (Disp)
2nd A-LOCK ⟦"⟧ **WHAT ⟦␣⟧ R** 2nd A-LOCK ⟦"⟧
ENTER
PRGM ▶ to I/O
2 (Input) ALPHA **R**
ENTER
2nd ⟦{x}⟧ **1** ⟦)⟧ STO▶ 2nd ⟦{y}⟧ **1** ⟦)⟧
ENTER
2 STO▶ **I**
ENTER
PRGM
ENTER ([b1) **2**
ENTER
ALPHA **R** 2nd ⟦{y}⟧ ALPHA **I** ⟦−⟧ **1** ⟦)⟧ ⟦+⟧ 2nd ⟦{x}⟧ ALPHA **I** ⟦)⟧
   STO▶ 2nd ⟦{y}⟧ ALPHA **I** ⟦)⟧
ENTER
PRGM ▶ to I/O
ENTER (Disp)
2nd ⟦{y}⟧ ALPHA **I** ⟦−⟧ **1** ⟦)⟧
ENTER
PRGM
4 (IS>() ALPHA **I** ALPHA **,** ALPHA **N** ⟦+⟧ **1** ⟦)⟧
ENTER
PRGM
2 (Goto) **2**

Synthetic Division continued

[ENTER]

[PRGM] [▶] to I/O

[ENTER] (Disp)

[2nd] [A-LOCK] ["] **REMAINDER** [2nd] [A-LOCK] ["]

[ENTER]

[PRGM] [▶] to I/O

[ENTER] (Disp)

[2nd] [{y}] [ALPHA] I [−] 1 [ )]

[ENTER]

[PRGM]

7 (End)

Program appears as:

Prgm S: SYNTH
: Clr Home
: Clr Stat
: Disp "POLY DEGREE"
: Input N
: Disp " "
: Disp "COEFFICIENTS"
: $\theta \rightarrow I$
: Lbl 1
: $N - I \rightarrow E$
: Disp E
: Input {x} (I + 1)
: IS > (I, N)
: Goto 1
: Disp "WHAT R"
: Input R
: {x} (1) → {y} (1)
: $2 \rightarrow I$
: Lbl 2
: R {y} (I − 1) + {x} (I) → {y} (I)
: Disp {y} (I − 1)
: IS > (I, N + 1)
: Goto 2
: Disp "REMAINDER"
: Disp {y} (I − 1)
: End

Note: A basic understanding of synthetic division is needed. For example, the student must know how to enter the coefficients of the polynomial (enter zero for missing terms) and must know that R is found by solving for x ($x − 2 = 0$, $x = 2 = R$). Then, the student must be able to state the answer correctly.

$$1$$
$$-3$$ is the calculator's answer for the example below.
remainder 0

The student must understand that these numbers are now the coefficients of the polynomial answer.

Example	$x^2 − 5x + 6 \div (x − 2)$
PRGM# (EXEC)	What R
Poly Degree	?**2** [ENTER]
? **2** [ENTER]	1
Coefficients	-3
? **1** [ENTER]	remainder 0
-5 [ENTER]	this means answer is x − 3
6 [ENTER]	to check, does (x − 2)(x − 3) = $x^2 − 5x + 6$? yes

Practice

1. $x^3 + 3x^2 − 2x − 8 \div (x + 2)$

2. $x^2 + 8x + 12 \div (x + 2)$

3. $x^3 + 2x + 3 \div (x − 2)$

4. $x^3 + x^2 − 17x + 15 \div (x + 5)$

5. $2x^3 − 2x − 3 \div (x − 1)$

6. $x^4 + x^3 − 1 \div (x − 2)$

7. $3x^4 − 2x^3 + 5x^2 − 4x − 2 \div (x + 1)$

Applications A

Name _____

OBJECTIVES: To use the programs on the TI-81 to solve the problems below

1. Is the triangle with vertices at $(1, 0)$, $(0, 2)$ and $(2, 3)$ isosceles?

2. Is the triangle with vertices at $(-6, -2)$, $(-5, 2)$ $(-3, 1)$ a right triangle? Explain your answer. Which program(s) did you use?

3. A pool is 14 m long and 11 m wide. A sidewalk of uniform width is placed around the pool. The area of the sidewalk is 116 square meters. What is the width of the border?

4. Find two consecutive positive integers whose product is 210.

5. Solve.
    $$x - 2y + 3z = 2$$
    $$2x - 3y + z = 1$$
    $$3x - y + 2z = 9$$

6. Solve.
    $$2x + 3y = -1$$
    $$5x - 2y = -12$$

7. The area of a rectangular court is 192 square meters. The length is 4 meters more than its width. Find the dimensions.

8. Factor $x^2 - 2x - 35$.

9. Factor $6x^2 - 5x - 4$.

10. Solve $15x^2 = -7x + 4$.

11. Find the perimeter of the square whose vertices are $(2, 1)$, $(7, 1)$, $(2, 16)$, $(7, 16)$.

12. The square of a number is 4 more than 3 times the number. Find the number.

13. A pool is twice as long as it is wide. Its area can be doubled by adding 3 meters to its length and one meter to its width. Find the dimensions of the pool.

Applications B

Name _____

OBJECTIVES: To use the programs on the TI-81 to solve the problems below

1. Thrice that is six less this. Twice this increased by what is four. If twice what is five less than that, find that, this and what! (Hint: Set up 3 equations using x, y and z for that, this and what.)

2. Solve.
$$2x + 3y = 6$$
$$2x - 5y = 22$$

3. Find the value of
$$\begin{vmatrix} 10 & 50 \\ -5 & 25 \end{vmatrix}$$

4. Solve.
$$x - 2y + z = 7$$
$$3x + y - z = 2$$
$$2x + 3y + 2z = 7$$

5. Solve.
$$2x + 6y + 8z = 5$$
$$-2x + 9y - 12z = -1$$
$$4x + 6y - 4z = 3$$

6. Graph the line $3x + 4y = 12$. Check it using your TI-81 graphing function. (Hint: Solve for y.)

7. Solve this system of equations using elimination. Then, graph each line on the same axes using your TI-81 and verify the point of intersection (solution).
$$2x - y = 4$$
$$x + y = 5$$

8. Graph these two lines using your TI-81 graphing calculator and estimate the point of intersection. Then, find the solution using the matrix program to verify the point.
$$3x - 2y = 12$$
$$4x + 2y = 2$$

74

Answer Key

page 2—Basic Numbers...

1	6	9	3			1	4	2
8		8	0	6	6			8
3			0		3	2	7	
9	9	9		4	0	2		
	5	0		2	0	2	5	
9	8	4		0		9	0	
4		1	8	0	5		0	
2	7		6	0	6	0	0	

page 4—You Write the Rules (Addition)

I.
1. -7	6. 15	11. 12
2. 8	7. 2	12. -4
3. 5	8. -12	13. 3
4. -5	9. 9	14. -10
5. 0	10. -19	15. -6

page 5—You Write the Rules (+)

II.
same	different
5 + 3 = 8	3 + -8 = 5
3 + 6 = 9	16 + -16 = 0
-11 + -8 = -19	-1 + 16 = 15
1 + 11 = 12	13 + -11 = 2
-2 + -2 = -4	5 + -17 = -12
-4 + -6 = -10	10 + -8 = 2
	-8 + 2 = -6

III.
1. a. Add the two numbers.
   b. same sign
2. a. Subtract the two numbers.
   b. take the sign of the larger number
3. a. add and keep the sign
   b. subtract and take the sign of the larger number

page 6—You Write the Rules (+)

B. 1. add and keep the sign
   2. subtract and take the sign of the larger number

page 3—Measuring Problems

1. Start both hourglasses at same time. When the 7-minute hourglass is empty, there will be four minutes left on the 11-minute hourglass. Start timing at this point. (It will take four minutes.) When it is empty, turn it over and let it run out (11 minutes). (4 + 11 = 15)

2. Fill the 13-gallon can with water. Pour out the 5-gallon can leaving 8 gallons. Pour this 8 gallons into the 11-gallon can. Repeat this to leave another 8 gallons in the 13-gallon can, which will leave the last 8 gallons in the 24-gallon can.

3. Divide the coins into 3 sets of 3 each and weigh two sets. 1) If they balance, the fake coin is in the remaining set of 3. Weigh two of these against each other. If they balance, the remaining coin is fake. If they do not balance, the lighter coin is the fake one. 2) If they don't balance, the fake coin is in the set of 3 that weighs less; then proceed as above with the 3 individual ones.

4. (Similar concept as #3) Divide coins into 3 sets of 4 each. In the first weighing, balance one set against another. This will determine (as in #3) which set of 4 contains the fake coin. Then do a second weighing (using the set with the fake coin)—2 against 2. One of these will contain the fake. Then, pick those two and weigh one against one.

5. One can of soda weighs as much as 5 boxes of popcorn.

page 7—You Write the Rules (x)

I.
same	different
-5 • -4 = 20	1 • -7 = -7
-3 • -4 = 12	-3 • 7 = -21
5 • 10 = 50	-4 • 3 = -12
2 • 8 = 16	3 • -4 = -12
-2 • -8 = 16	-5 • 4 = -20
	-7 • 3 = -21
	8 • -8 = -64
	7 • -1 = -7

II.
1. a. positive
   b. no
   c. no
2. a. negative
   b. no
   c. no
3. a. positive
   b. negative

page 8—You Write the Rules (÷)

I.
1. 6 ÷ 3 = 2	9. -20 ÷ 4 = -5
2. -6 ÷ 2 = -3	10. -21 ÷ 3 = -7
3. 20 ÷ -4 = -5	11. -64 ÷ -8 = 8
4. -7 ÷ 1 = -7	12. -7 ÷ -1 = 7
5. -21 ÷ -3 = 7	13. 50 ÷ 10 = 5
6. 12 ÷ -4 = -3	14. 16 ÷ 8 = 2
7. -12 ÷ 3 = -4	15. 16 ÷ -8 = -2
8. -12 ÷ -4 = 3	

same	different
6 ÷ 3 = 2	-6 ÷ 2 = -3
-21 ÷ -3 = 7	20 ÷ -4 = -5
-12 ÷ -4 = 3	-7 ÷ 1 = -7
-64 ÷ -8 = 8	12 ÷ -4 = -3
-7 ÷ -1 = 7	-12 ÷ 3 = -4
50 ÷ 10 = 5	-20 ÷ 4 = -5
16 ÷ 8 = 2	-21 ÷ 3 = -7
	16 ÷ -8 = -2

II. 1. positive
    2. negative

page 9—You Write the Rules (x and ÷)

A.

-6	8	(14)	-2	(-16)	12	-20	2	-4	-10
(6)	-12	21	3	-24	-18	(-30)	-3	(5)	15
-15	20	-35	-5	40	(-30)	-50	5	-10	-25
(33)	44	-77	-11	88	66	-110	11	-22	(55)

1. 3 x 3 = 9
2. 3 x -11 = -33
3. 7 x -2 = -14
4. -8 x -2 = 16
5. -6 x -5 = 30
6. 10 x 3 = 30
7. 2 x 3 = 6
8. 5 x -11 = -55

B.

1. -4
2. -1
3. -16
4. 150
5. 13
6. -2
7. 8
8. -7
9. 21
10. 2
11. -15
12. 1
13. 215
14. 13
15. -14
16. 1
17. -7
18. -33

C. I hear math is fun and easy, do you think so? I love math!

page 10—Other Rules...

1. a. add and keep the sign
   b. subtract and take the sign of the larger
2. a. answer will be positive
   b. answer will be negative
3. a. 3 + 0 = 3, Additive Identity, 8 + 0 = 8
   b. -5 • -1/5 = 1, Multiplicative Inverse, 8 • 1/8 = 1
   c. -6 + 6 = 0, Additive Inverse, 5 + -5 = 0
   d. 1 • -17 = -17, Multiplicative Identity, 2 • 1 = 2
   e. 5 – 3 = 5 + -3 = 2, Subtraction, -8 – -3 = -8 + 3 = -5
   f. 71 • 0 = 0, Zero Multiplication, -11 • 0 = 0
4. a. grouping symbols
   b. multiplication and division (left to right)
   c. addition and subtraction (left to right)

page 11—Number Practice

1. -226
2. 78
3. 2
4. 0
5. -93
6. -19
7. 11
8. 777
9. -29
10. -513
11. -7
12. -625
13. -16
14. 5
15. -5
16. -120
17. 300
18. -18
19. 9
20. -560
21. -12
22. 0
23. 1
24. -1,728
25. -243
26. 9
27. -6
28. 16
29. 30
30. 2
31. 0
32. -87
33. -12
34. 4,096
35. 1
36. 0
37. 1
38. -810
39. -2
40. 0

page 13—Evaluating...

-1	2		-1	4	4		-2	3
1	0		1	0	4		3	2
6	4						6	8
	-7	2		-3	7			
3	3						-4	2
8	9		-1	1	3		2	4
4	5		1	0	8		5	3

page 14—
What's the Number?

1. 4 brothers, 3 sisters
2. 42 is the missing number; pattern = first number times two plus the second number
3.

0	12	12	0
8	4	4	8
4	8	8	4
12	0	0	12

4. a. 28 triangles
   b. 16 triangles
5. 27 regular hexagons

C.

	pencils	erasers	rulers	amount of change
5th	12	1	0	24
4th	2	1	2	12
3rd	2	13	1	0
2nd	6	6	1	4
1st	3	5	1	26

page 16—Number Patterns...

A.

item	1	2	3	4	5	6	7	8	9	10
eraser	4¢	8¢	12¢	16¢	20¢	24¢	28¢	32¢	36¢	40¢
pencil	6¢	12¢	18¢	24¢	30¢	36¢	42¢	48¢	54¢	60¢
compass	25¢	50¢	75¢	100¢	125¢	150¢	175¢	200¢	225¢	250¢
ruler	36¢	72¢	108¢	144¢	180¢	216¢	252¢	288¢	324¢	360¢

B.
1. 6 erasers, 4 pencils
   3 erasers, 6 pencils
   0 erasers, 8 pencils
   9 erasers, 2 pencils
2. Answers will vary.

page 17—
Number Puzzlers I

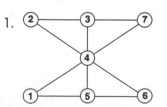

1.
2.
3. 29
4. 156
5.

Answer Key

page 18—Number Puzzlers II   (Answers may vary.)

1.

2.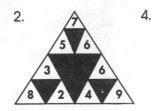

4.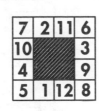

page 19—The "Ultimate..."

	A	B	C	D
I	5	7	6	2
II	3	2	8	5
III	6	4	1	3
IV	1	8	7	4

page 20—Just for Fun! (A)

1.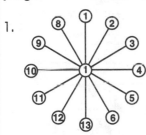

2.

3.
7	2	9
8	6	4
3	10	5

4.
	3	5	
7	1	8	2
	4	6	

5.
```
•  •  •
•  •  •
•  •  •
```

page 21—Numbers,...

1.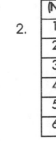

2.
(N)	(S)
1	1
2	4
3	9
4	16
5	25
6	36

Pattern = $N^2 = S$

3. The (tired) ant had traveled 19 feet when it reached the top of the last step.

4.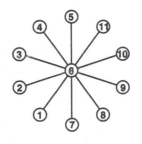

page 22—Equation-Solving "Flow Chart"

1.
$$x + 3 = -5$$
(#4) $x + 3 + -3 = -5 + -3$
$$\mathbf{x = -8}$$
$-8 + 3 = -5 \;\checkmark$

2. (#5) $\dfrac{2x}{2} = \dfrac{10}{2}$
$$\mathbf{x = 5}$$
$2(5) = 10 \;\checkmark$

3.
$$2x + 4 = 18$$
(#4) $2x + 4 + -4 = 18 + -4$
(#5) $\dfrac{2x}{2} = \dfrac{14}{2}$
$$\mathbf{x = 7}$$
$2(7) + 4 = 18 \;\checkmark$

4.
$$2(x - 3) = 24$$
(#1) $2(x + -3) = 24$
(#2) $2x + -6 = 24$
(#4) $2x + -6 + 6 = 24 + 6$
(#5) $\dfrac{2x}{2} = \dfrac{20}{2}$
$$\mathbf{x = 15}$$
$2(15 - 3) = 24 \;\checkmark$

5.
$$7 = 6x + 19$$
(#3) $6x + 19 = 7$
(#4) $6x + 19 + -19 = 7 + -19$
(#5) $\dfrac{6x}{6} = \dfrac{-12}{6}$
$$\mathbf{x = -2}$$
$7 = 6(-2) + 19 \;\checkmark$

6.
$$^2/_3x + 5 = 23$$
(#4) $^2/_3x + 5 + -5 = 23 + -5$
(#5) $^2/_3x = 18$
$^3/_2 \cdot {}^2/_3x = 18 \cdot {}^3/_2$
$$\mathbf{x = 27}$$
$^2/_3(27) + 5 = 23 \;\checkmark$

7.
$$-3x + 6(x - 4) = 9$$
(#1) $-3x + 6(x + -4) = 9$
(#2) $-3x + 6x + -24 = 9$
$3x + -24 = 9$
(#4) $3x + -24 + 24 = 9 + 24$
(#5) $\dfrac{3x}{3} = \dfrac{33}{3}$
$$\mathbf{x = 11}$$
$-3(11) + 6(11 - 4) = 9 \;\checkmark$

8.
$$3(2x + 1) = -15$$
(#2) $6x + 3 = -15$
(#4) $6x + 3 + -3 = -15 + -3$
(#5) $\dfrac{6x}{6} = \dfrac{-18}{6}$
$$\mathbf{x = -3}$$
$3(2(-3) + 1) = -15 \;\checkmark$

page 23—Applications...

1. 9, 12
2. 18, 90
3. 9, 36
4. 13, 18
5. 8, 17
6. 93, 20
7. 24, 6, 15
8. 10, 20, 19
9. 19, 10
10. 4, 9
11. 8, 2

page 24—Applications...

1. 17 cm x 10 cm
2. 29 cm x 12 cm
3. a = 9 cm; b = 6 cm; c = 11 cm
4. 14 in., 14 in., 4 in.
5. 157 m x 43 m
6. 950 m, 700 m, 850 m

Answer Key

page 25—Equation...

3	5		2	9	4
5		3			2
6	0	2		6	0
		2	3.	4	
2.	4		0		3
7		1	8		9

page 28—Think...

1. 1. d
   2. c
   3. a
   4. b
2. 19 athletes
3. 90 points

page 29—Factoring x²...

(x + 4)	(x + 12)			(x + 4)	(x + 4)			(x − 6)	(x + 4)
(x − 6)			(x − 5)	(x + 5)			(x − 9)	(x − 2)	(x − 4)
	(x + 3)				(x − 8)	(x + 4)			
(x + 10)	(x + 10)		(x + 10)	(x + 2)				(x − 6)	(x − 3)
		(x − 4)	(x − 6)					(x + 5)	
(x + 6)	(x + 2)	(x + 12)		(x + 3)	(x + 3)				(x − 6)
(x − 8)	(x + 12)		(x − 7)	(x + 7)			(x + 5)	(x − 9)	

page 26—Equation Fun

page 31—Consecutive...

1. 22, 24
2. 11, 13
3. 7, 9
4. 10, 11 and -11, -10
5. -7, -6
6. 4, 6, 8

page 30—Factoring ax² + bx + c

(2x −3)	(2x + 1)			(x + 4)	(2x + 1)			(3x − 4)	(2x − 1)
(3x + 2)			(x − 3)	(3x + 2)		(2x + 1)	(2x + 3)	(2x − 3)	
	(3x + 4)				(3x − 1)	(3x + 4)			
(3x − 1)	(2x + 1)		(2x + 3)	(2x + 5)			(4x + 1)	(x + 3)	
	(3x − 2)	(3x + 2)					(2x + 5)		
(3x + 4)	(2x − 5)	(3x + 2)		(4x + 1)	(x − 4)			(3x + 4)	
(2x − 5)	(3x − 1)		(3x − 2)	(2x + 3)			(2x − 3)	(2x + 3)	

page 32— Factoring Uses!

1. (x + 3)
2. (x − 2)
3. x² + 9x + 18
4. (x + 5) by (x − 5)
5. 12' x 15'
6. 4 x 7
7. 3 x 5
8. 4 = height
   12 = base
9. side = 6
10. side = 2

page 33—Equation...

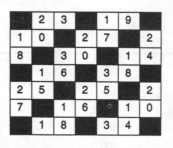

page 36—Ordered Pairs

I. A (3, 3)
B (-4, 2)
C (-3, -3)
D (4, -2)
E (3, 0)
F (0, -3)
G (-2, 0)
H (0, 4)

II. A)
1. (4, 1)
2. (-7, -1)
3. (1, 3)
4. (-2, -4)
5. (0, -1)
6. (5, -1)

B)
1. (1, 4)
2. (3, -5)
3. (1, -1)
4. (6, 2)
5. (0, 4)
6. (10, 9)
7. (-5, -1)
8. (5, -1)

page 34— Combination...

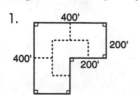

pages 37-38

A.

C	C	C	D	D
G	G	C	D	D
B	A	A	F	F
B	B	A	A	F
B	H	E	E	E

B.

E	H	A	B	C	C
E	A	A	B	B	C
E	A	G	B	I	C
D	D	G	F	I	I
D	D	F	F	I	I

page 39—Shape Up!

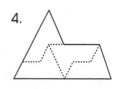

pages 40-41 What Comes Next?

A. 1. A   3. A   5.   6. ■
   2. E   4. C

B. 1. C   3. D   5. ⊥   6.
   2. D   4. B

page 42—Shape Splitters

1.
400'
400'
200'
200'

2.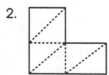

3.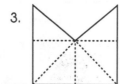

4.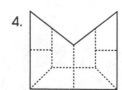

5. Form a tetrahedron

page 43—Moving Magic (A)

1.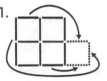

2. a. 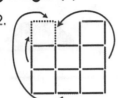 c.

   b. (triangles) d. (triangles)

3. Answers will vary. One possibility is:

4. Answers will vary.

5. Move the horizontal toothpick ¹/₂ length to the right and the upper left toothpick to the lower right position.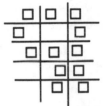

page 44—Moving Magic (B)

1.   2.   3. start   4. 1

5. 60 rpm, clockwise

page 45—Just for Fun! (B)

1. Answers will vary.

2. 27—16 △ 7 △ 3 △ 1 △

3. Answers will vary.

4. Answers may vary.

page 49—Company Communication

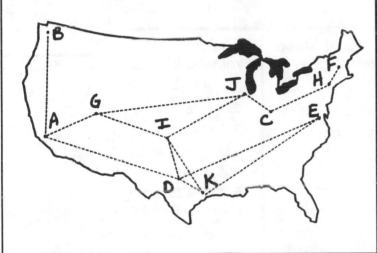

page 48—Logic (Survey)

Name	Subject	Location	Day
Pat	Politics	Bank	Wed
Linda	Newspapers	Town Hall	Fri
Terri	Electronics	Mall	Thur
Paula	TV	Train Station	Tues
Sam	Food Labeling	Bus Stop	Mon

5.   6.   7.

8. (tangram) 9. (tangram) 10. (tangram)

pages 53-56—Tangrams

1.   2.   3. (tangram) 4.

11. (tangram) 12. (tangram) 13. (tangram) 14. (tangram) 15. (tangram) 16. (tangram)

22.

17. (tangram) 18. (tangram) 19. (tangram) 20. (tangram) 21. (tangram) 23.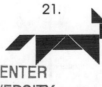

79

pages 53-56—Tangrams

24.
25.
26.
27.
28.
29.
30.
31.
32.
33.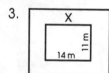
34.
35.
36.
37.
38.
39.
40.

---

page 65—Matrices A

1. 15   4. 0
2. -90   5. -93
3. 1   6. -890

page 66—Matrices B

1. $(-2, -8)$
2. $(4, -2)$
3. $(1, 0)$
4. $x - 2y = 8$
   $4x - y = -3$
   $(-2, -5)$
5. $(-1.5, -1)$
6. $(7, 1.5)$
7. $(-5, 5)$
8. $(3, -2)$
9. $(3, 2, 1)$
10. $(-2, 1, 3)$
11. $(-1, 3, 0.5)$

page 68—Distance...

1. 8.5
2. 6.4
3. 2.2
4. 7.8
5. 5.8

---

page 69—Quadratic Formula

1. $x = 3, x = 4$
2. $x = -1, x = 9$
3. $x = -5, x = -2$
4. $x = -0.5, x = 3$
5. $x = -^2/_3 (-0.\overline{6})$, $x = -0.5$
6. $x = -1$
7. $x = 1, x = 5$
8. $x = -5, x = -1.5$
9. $x = -0.5, x = 4$
10. $x = -^3/_5 (-0.6), x = 9$

page 70—Area of Triangles

1. 6
2. 210
3. 9.9
4. 6.5

page 72—Synthetic Division

1. $x^2 + x - 4$
2. $x + 6$
3. $x^2 + 2x + 6 + \dfrac{15}{x - 2}$
4. $x^2 - 4x + 3$
5. $2x^2 + 2x + \dfrac{-3}{x - 1}$
6. $x^3 + 3x^2 + 6x + 12 + \dfrac{23}{x - 2}$
7. $3x^3 - 5x^2 + 10x - 14 + \dfrac{12}{x + 1}$

---

page 73—Applications A

1. Yes.
2. No.
3.

	x	
		11 m
14 m		

   $(2x + 11)(2x + 14) = 270$
   $4x^2 + 50x - 116 = 0$
   Use Quadform program.
   $x = 2$
   width of border = 2
4. 14, 15
5. $(3, 2, 1)$
6. $(-2, 1)$
7. 12×16
8. $(x - 7)(x + 5)$
9. $(2x + 1)(3x - 4)$

10. $x = -^4/_5 (-0.8)$, $x = ^1/_3 (0.\overline{3})$
11. 40 units
12. $x = -1$ or $x = 4$
13. $2(2x^2) = (x + 1)(2x + 3)$
    answer is 3 x 6

page 74—Applications B

1. $3x = 6 - y$
   $2y + z = 4$ $(1, 3, -2)$
   $2z = x - 5$
2. $(6, -2)$
3. 500
4. $(2, -1, 3)$
5. $(^1/_2, ^1/_3, ^1/_4)$
6.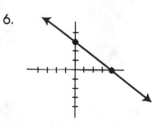
7. $(3, 2)$
8. $(2, -3)$
